5 SIMPLE STEPS TO WEALTH

5 SIMPLE STEPS TO WEALTH

The Five Step Plan You Need To Take To Get Ahead
Financially

TRACEY EDWARDS

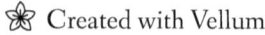 Created with Vellum

Contents

Start At The Beginning

INTRODUCTION

THE GIRL WATCHED her mother's hands shake as she placed the three bowls of pink rice on the table. It belied her smile as she sat down in front of one of the bowls and said "yum".

The boy, younger than his sister, made a face as he stared at his dinner. The same meal as last night, except then it was blue. Maybe it was the color pink, or maybe that he was sick of eating rice. It was the third time that week.

To an outsider, it would have been clear that the mother was having a particularly tough week. To feed her family she had resorted to using food coloring in the rice water to make it seem different than the previous day.

To anyone who asked, the girl would have said that the pink rice was definitely better than the blue. No-one ever asked.

Years went by and the girl was in high school. Public of course because no-one she knew ever went to private school. A new kid in the year above was drawing a crowd and the girl made her way over to see what was going on.

He was different from most of the other kids at the school as his father owned a business and they lived in a big house at the edge of town. This particular day he had purchased a lot of food from the school canteen. But he wasn't eating it. To the amusement of many of the other children, he laughed as he threw the food at the wall, watching as it exploded onto the bricks.

The girl didn't laugh. The girl was horrified at the wastefulness of it. To spend money on something that was gone without anyone benefiting. He clearly didn't know his crowd. The other students might have laughed, but she saw their gaze linger on the mess on the ground. Food that could have filled any of their stomachs.

If that was what having money meant, being wasteful and foolish, she would have none of it. She preferred her mothers way of stretching a dollar and appreciating what you had.

I DON'T RECALL what happened in my mother's life that particular week that she fed my brother and I rice or why it was different from any other, although living frugally was a necessary way of life then.

I always knew the power of money, but then it was simply how not to waste it. I believed those that had money were foolish with it. I never wanted to be a fool.

This idea of money was challenged when I entered the workforce.

A young man came into my life. He came from a family that was well-off financially. I was unsure about him at first, but he was generous, sweet, and funny which made me intrigued.

He took me to restaurants and bought me gifts. But not in an extravagant show-off way. He knew what he could afford and wanted to enjoy life. He wanted me to appreciate these gifts for the time and thought he put into them, rather than boast about how much they cost.

Even though it didn't last, (we were both too young for anything serious), he changed my thoughts on money very quickly. Having money didn't mean one was a bad person, after all. A person is who they are regardless of what they have. You could appreciate things with money, just as much as without.

From that moment on I was curious about who I would be if I had money. Would it change me? How would it impact the way I lived? Would I still be nice or, like the boy in high school, wasteful?

But mostly I wanted to know if it was possible. Could I go from having nothing to becoming wealthy?

I was on a mission to find out.

I started budgeting and saving at first—where most people start when they want to change their finances. It was a good foundation, but I could see that it wasn't getting me that far. I didn't know what to do next.

I read books and studied others who'd gotten rich and how they'd done it. Mostly it was though large businesses. A few had done it through property investing. Then I found a new book that started me on my journey to financial independence.

It was about Warren Buffett. He'd gotten rich through the stock market. Something, at the time, I knew little about. But I was intrigued.

I'd done a year of finance at university before switching to journalism. I liked numbers and was good at them. So I read everything I could about stocks and how to invest. That was the missing piece to my puzzle on how to get rich. It was a numbers game. Profit and losses on a spreadsheet. It suited me well.

Maybe in this book, you'll find something that resonates with you. It doesn't have to be the stock market. Everyone's path is different.

I've covered everything I know on how to take you on the journey to a better financial future.

We start at the beginning.

Step One is creating a foundation of tracking spending and starting a budget. You need to know where you are before you can proceed to somewhere new.

Step Two will give you tips to curb your spending. Not to deny anything you love, but to make room for it.

Step Three offers tips on getting out of debt. Bad debt is a burden that causes too much stress and not something we need in our lives. Not if we want a brighter future.

Step Four is starting a savings plan. From building an emergency fund to having enough money to cover all those yearly expenses. Then you can start saving for the fun stuff because everything else will be taken care of.

And lastly, Step Five, is investing. It might not be the stock market for you, although I do have a chapter on that. It might be property or business or just investing in yourself. We all have different goals and different needs in life. Investing just means making your money work for you in whichever way you want.

I've included all the action steps at the end of this book in an easy to refer to list.

It's a simple path to get you from where you are now to where you want to be in the future. Most people over complicate their finances. It doesn't have to be that way. Keep it simple and take the steps one by one.

It won't be easy though. Just because something is simple doesn't mean it won't take hard work.

But I know you can do it. You've already taken a step by buying this book.

Now let's take the next one and begin our journey to wealth.

STEP ONE - CREATE YOUR BUDGET

What you'll learn in this section:

- The budgeting method best suited to you.
- Whether to use a spreadsheet, app, or paper journal.
- Why it doesn't matter where you start, as long as you start (and add to it as you progress).
- The steps for setting up your budget.
- How to keep it up to date.

Why Have A Budget?

ANYONE WHO IS STARTING a journey knows that before you leave you need to know where you are. It takes knowing point A if you want to get to point B.

Once you know where you are, you can create a plan to get to your destination. The destination is a better financial future. Our starting point is right here.

But do you know where you are financially right now? Do you have exact figures on what you spend, how much income is coming in, and where your money is going?

Maybe you do. Maybe you're one of the few people who has a working budget and sticks to it. If so, you can skip to the next section.

But if you don't, if you're only guessing at your income and expenses, it's time to find out.

Everybody needs some kind of budget. It's a bold statement, I know, but it's the one thing which all financial experts agree. You have to know how much money is coming in, and how much money is going out.

That's true whether you're in business or a regular person like you or me.

If the key to getting ahead financially is spending less than you earn. Another thing that all financial experts agree on. Then you have to know what those figures are, for you.

And that means writing it down somewhere.

Yet according to a 2013 Gallup Poll [source: http://news.gallup.com/poll/162872/one-three-americans-prepare-detailed-household-budget.aspx] only about one-third of people have a budget.

The remaining two-thirds either try to budget in their heads or don't think about it much at all.

Easy come, easy go, right?

Unfortunately, that lack of planning can get people into financial problems without them even realizing it.

Have you ever looked at your credit card statement and asked yourself: *Why is it so much? What on earth did I buy?*

It's easy to overspend when you aren't sure what you have allocated to spend.

By tracking your spending and income you can easily create a budget that's tailored specifically for you and your situation.

And by having a budget you'll see at one glance how much money you have for paying off debts (if you have any), how much you can save (for something you love), and how much you can spend (we all need some discretionary income). It encompasses three of the five steps to building long-term wealth.

———

KEY TAKEAWAY

A budget will let you see all your income and expenses

in one place so that you can make choices and allocate your money where it needs to go.

It will allow you to manage your money so you can gain control over your finances and start building wealth.

Understanding How You Budget

KNOW YOUR BUDGETING PERSONALITY

EVERYBODY HAS a different idea of what a budget is. Especially because there are so many different types of personal budgets.

Most agree that it's a way of understanding your finances. Some see it as constraining or limiting, whereas others enjoy the clarity it brings. Some follow the rules of their preferred method to a T, whereas others tweak and adapt one to suit their circumstances.

All a budget really is, is a tool to track your spending and expenses, and know what income you have to pay for everything.

Budgets can be as simple or as complicated as you like.

Don't let anyone tell you that there is only one way to do one.

There are as many styles of budgets as there are personalities. The trick is knowing which style of budgeting is going to work for you.

If you've ever given up on a budget, it was probably because it didn't suit your style. You are far more likely to stick with one if it suits you. So know thyself and what you are most likely to use.

There are different methods, and I'm going to explore two of the most common ones in the next chapter, but first, you need to figure out how you're going to record your budget.

Spreadsheet/Paper/App — Which Budget Style is Best?

The three most common ways to keep track of your budget are:

- Using a spreadsheet.
- Writing it down on paper.
- Using a budgeting app or program.

Most of these can be customized to fit your needs

although making your own budget is more flexible than using a set program or app.

Neither is better than the other, it's just what you prefer.

The Spreadsheet Budget

A spreadsheet is what I use. Probably because I'm used to using Excel all those years I worked in an office environment. There's something I like about letting the spreadsheet perform all the math and all I have to do is enter the details.

If you don't have Excel use Google Sheets. It's free and pretty much the same. Plus you can access your budget from your computer or phone making it easy to update whenever you need to.

My spreadsheet is simple. I have two sections.

The first is for income. I input all the money I made for that month which might include book sales, blog advertising, affiliate marketing, dividends and bank interest.

I don't earn a regular income, it varies month to month. But this works whether you have multiple streams like I do or just one paycheck.

Budgeting on a single income makes things a lot easier

because you always know what's coming in. No surprises.

The second section is for my expenses. I have a row for rent, groceries, takeout food, general shopping/entertainment, petrol/gas/transport, internet, phone, household bills (utilities), and so on.

If I need to, it's easy to add a new row for a one-off miscellaneous expense or even make a new category if it becomes regular.

My budget is always being tweaked as my needs change because of how varied my income and expenses are.

The Paper Budget

If you're more down with keeping it no-tech, using a paper budget is the way to go. It's been proven that physically writing things down helps your brain better process the information too.

You could start with a blank page in a new notepad, create your budget in a bullet journal, or use a myriad of downloadable budget sheets you find online.

I do a very quick budget plan on paper before each month starts, forecasting what my expenses and income are likely to be. (I keep exact amounts in my spreadsheet). It's usually pretty close because I've been tracking my expenses and income for a while, but every now and then I get unexpected expenses or, better, income.

Budgeting on paper keeps things simple and uncomplicated. It can be as pretty or practical as you prefer. Plus you don't have to rely on wifi or battery power to check in.

Have a journal or notepad that's specifically for your finances.

It can be any size, but if you plan on taking it with you to write down all your expenses as you make them, it needs to be small enough to be portable. If you're just leaving it at home, size isn't as important.

Using a Budgeting App or Program

I don't use a budgeting program because most of the ones I've used in the past have been too restricting or complicated. Or I've just got bored with them and returned to using paper or spreadsheets instead.

But if you're the type to keep things high tech then an app or program is the way to go.

With some apps/programs, you can link them to your

bank accounts and credit cards so that they'll track your spending for you without you having to do anything. Some also give tips where you are overspending.

In the USA, Mint is considered one of the best budgeting apps. In Australia, Pocketbook is pretty popular. Both are free for the basic version, but you can upgrade to the paid version to access more features.

I don't have an opinion on either one because I've not used them, but if they are something you'd like to try there are plenty of reviews online to help make up your mind.

———

TAKE ACTION

Decide whether you're going to use a spreadsheet, journal, or app for your budget.

You'll start creating your actual budget soon, but first you need to decide how you are going to record your income and expenses.

The most common ways are either paper, app, or spreadsheet program. Which do you prefer?

Two Popular Budgeting Methods

THE REVERSE BUDGET AND THE ZERO-BASED BUDGET

NOW THAT YOU'VE decided how you're going to get those numbers down, let's look at two popular budgeting methods being used right now.

Both have fans that say the method works for them, so it's working out which one suits you best.

The two are the Reverse Budget and the Zero-Based Budget. Let's look at them in more detail:

The Reverse Budget (or Backward Budget)

The reverse budget or budgeting in reverse is what I first used when I had a more stable income. It can be done with any income, both fixed and variable.

Instead of calculating your fixed expenses and spending

money, and then allocating what's left to your savings, you take out your savings first.

You've probably heard it as "pay yourself first". That's what this is.

Most people who say they can't save, spend first and then save what's left over. Unfortunately, there's never any money left over.

With budgeting in reverse, you determine a set amount of money to save each paycheck. And if you have debts, you set this up first too.

Then once your savings have been taken out and moved to a high-interest savings account which I'll talk about in Step Four, and you've paid the amounts off your debt, you pay for your fixed expenses—that's your rent/mortgage, food, bills, etc. You can automate this as much as possible to make it easier.

Finally, whatever money is left over is your spending money. Because everything else is already taken care of, you're free to spend that money as you like.

The basic premise is: savings and debt first, then expenses, blow what's left.

No guilt, no worries.

The Zero-Based Budget

The zero-based budget is a method where you allocate every cent of your income to something. If you have $4,000 in income each month, you allocate all four grand of that to all your expenses, saving, and investing, leaving you with a balance sheet of zero. Income minus expenses equals zero.

It's not that you have nothing left at the end of the month (you are still allocating money to saving and investing and so on), but that each penny that you earn is accounted for.

This method of budgeting is very similar to how most businesses operate. It's a simplified personal version of an accounting balance sheet.

The zero-based budget takes a little more planning than the backward budget because you need to allocate all your money somewhere. If your balance sheet doesn't equal zero you need to figure out why. Have $50 left over? Allocate it somewhere. Savings, debt reduction, spending, doesn't matter. Just keep it tracked.

Which is the Best Budget?

The best budget is the one that you'll use.

The truth is there is no *best* budget. Budgets aren't (and shouldn't be) a one-size-fits-all approach. They should help you get ahead with your finances and not constrict you.

If you're more detail oriented you might create a zero-based budget in your spreadsheet program. If you prefer to get the saving and expenses out of the way first so you can spend the rest, the reverse budget is probably more your style.

The Hybrid Budget

Personally, I prefer a hybrid approach. The hybrid budget is where you take a little bit of both of the above two budgets taking what works for you and what doesn't. Use what works, scrap the rest.

I track all my spending and expenses but I don't have individual categories for everything. Some things are lumped into one group simply called shopping. I also don't have a set amount of savings.

My method is to be mindful of my spending and whatever money I have left over at the end of the month is how much I put into savings or investments.

It works for me because I do have money left over. I'm

not a big spender. But if I did like spending money, then I'd lean toward a reverse budget (which is what I used previously).

Hack That Budget

The point is that you need to make whichever budgeting method you prefer work for you. Whichever one you choose, make it your own.

Your expenses, income, lifestyle, and circumstances are unlikely to be the same as anyone else.

Your budget is designed to fit your situation. Don't be afraid to add, remove, change the categories. Whatever works.

Change the layout, color code it, create pie charts, keep it in your back pocket. Modify the look, layout, and method until it fits you.

Don't settle for a generic budget when you can tailor it to fit your exact needs.

Hack that budget until it works for you.

———

TAKE ACTION

The two most popular budgeting methods are the reverse budget and the zero-based budget. Choose the one you like best.

The ***reverse budget*** (or backward budget) is the method where you pay yourself first. This means putting money into savings and paying off debts before you pay your expenses. Once you've done that you are free to spend the remainder.

1. Pay any debts
2. Add money to your savings.
3. Pay your monthly expenses.
4. You're free to spend what's left.

For the ***zero-based budget*** you allocate all of your money somewhere. It's more common for businesses to use, but it's popularity is growing with everyday people. The goal is to make sure every cent is accounted for.

1. The zero-based budget works best in a spreadsheet program or app. (It's harder to do on paper).
2. Your income goes at the top.

3. Decide where your income is going. Bills, savings, insurance, etc.
4. The goal is to allocate all of your income to all of your expenses and savings so you are left with a zero balance.

Time To Set Up The Budget

HAVING a budget is an excellent start to building wealth, but what if you haven't been shown how to stick to a budget?

Budgets might come naturally to some people, but it actually isn't common for most people to use one.

That's why most people don't.

But instead of focusing on why people fail (which isn't helpful to anyone), let's try and come up with a plan on how to make whichever budget method you've chosen succeed.

Plus, I'll give you some tips to keep your motivation going so you will want to make it part of your lifestyle.

Know the Goal

The goal of your budget is to make sure you have more income coming in than expenses going out — to live below your means. We've established that.

And while it sounds simple in theory, for many people it's not quite so easy.

Often people feel that if they just had more money that it would make things easier, and sure, more income definitely can help.

But finding more income is harder to come by than simply lowering your expenses. You will have far more control over what you already have rather than finding extra money every month.

Let's start where you are right now.

Step One: Put On Your Favorite Music

Whether you are starting your budget for the first time or you're a seasoned budgeter, I always think that when you have to do anything that seems like a chore (housework, cooking, budgeting), having background music makes it better.

Do a search on Spotify or YouTube for music playlists of

the artists or genres that you're into. Or just play your favorite mp3 (or LP if you're old-school).

Some people like ambient music, others prefer pop rock. I'm a bit of a nostalgia hits fan myself.

Now the beat is rocking, you're good to go.

Step Two: Set Up Your Budget

The first time that you set up your budget is the longest time that you'll spend on it. But still, you're probably only looking at half an hour or less to set it up.

After that, you'll tweak as you go, but it shouldn't take you any more than ten to fifteen minutes to update each week. Knowing that it won't take long will mean you will be able to make time for it.

You'll need one section for your income and another one for your expenses. If you know the amounts now you can add them in, but it's fine if you don't.

Just get in the main income and expenses that you remember. You can add the others as they occur over the next few weeks.

Step Three: Keep Your Budget Current

Keeping your budget up to date is really the key to make it work for you. That way you'll always have a good idea of where you are financially on any given day.

You don't need to know to the exact decimal point, but having an overall idea of how much you can spend without issue is important.

Choose a day to update your budget with expenses and income. How often you do this depends on the regularity of your income and expenses.

That could be daily, weekly or monthly.

I like weekly. At the end of each week, I go through and enter my expenses into whatever category they belong. Rent, shopping, food, etc. I also note any income I received that week.

I track those expenses and income so that when I'm forecasting for the following month I have a pretty good idea of what's normal for me and if I need to tweak any categories.

This is also the time that I pay any credit card expenses that show up on my statement if I haven't already done so. I keep a zero balance on my card as often as I can.

Doing it this way I can see quickly if I need to cut back, or if I can afford to splurge a little. The key is knowing what you have to work with and adjusting that based on your lifestyle. That's why tracking income and expenses is so powerful.

For example, if I notice that my grocery budget is creeping up higher than normal then I can cut back the following week by searching for budget options, plan meals from the freezer/pantry, or see what items at the supermarket are on sale that week.

A note about paying bills

Most bills come electronically now through email, although I still get some in the regular mail.

I tend to pay bills as they come in and tag the emails with a specific colored flag in my email client so I can find them easily at the end of the week. Paper bills (which I get rarely) are put on my desk where I can't miss them.

If I'm busy and can't pay the bill right away I set up a reminder to pay the bill in either my calendar or to-do app.

For large bills, like car insurance, that come less frequently there are three options:

Pay it all and be frugal for the rest of the month (fine if you have a good income-to-expenses ratio—sometimes this works for me), use savings (what I generally do if I can't pay in full from my income that month), or put installments away to cover the bill when it comes due with a yearly expenses fund (works best for those with fixed incomes). I'll be talking about a yearly expenses fund in the savings section later.

There is no right or wrong way to do it, it depends on your income and preference.

People with variable incomes may find they are able to pay the bill in full if it was a good income month or use savings as a backup. Fixed incomes tend to work better by saving installments into a yearly expenses fund.

Step Four: Stay Motivated

You might find that after the initial excitement of setting up your budget and tracking your spending that you start to lose interest.

Perhaps a week will go by and you forget to write something down, or you go on vacation and the budget plan starts to slip.

This can also happen when you don't see any progress being made and start to distrust the process and time it takes.

It's a bit like a diet. You don't see any progress at first and it can be discouraging, but like a diet, if you stick with it, it can change your life.

For that kick of motivation, social media can be a great source of inspiration. You can find tips and tricks for sticking with your budget, case studies of people who have rid themselves of huge amounts of debt, groups of people who are in a similar place in their lives as you.

If Pinterest is your thing, start a budgeting board and pin tips that inspire you. It doesn't have to be only budgeting tips either, you can pin quotes, pictures of things you want to save for, finance books you want to read.

Follow financially inspiring Instagrammers to see how they live their lives. Some will be frugal and minimal, others will be lavish and extravagant. Everyone's different. Just a tip though, don't become weak to the pretty things they have/show. Instagram pictures (just like other social media) can often be an illusion.

Join Facebook groups that encourage members with words or challenges. Find ones that are positive rather than filled with drama. You want motivation and truth. They are out there.

Go to YouTube to watch videos about money tips and ideas. There are plenty of great personal finance YouTubers on the platform. Even, *cough*, me.

Why Having a Budget and Tracking Expenses Works

The beauty of reviewing your budget every week (or month) is that you become accountable. If you know you'll be reviewing your purchases to enter into your budget it makes those snap decisions less likely.

Saving money becomes easier because you are mindful of your purchases going forward.

Kakeibo

There is a Japanese money saving technique called Kakeibo that claims to cut your spending by up to thirty-five percent. It's been around for more than one hundred years.

Its main principle is that you record everything you spend into a household ledger. The idea being that by tracking what you spend, you become more mindful of your future purchases.

Relying on memory to determine a budget is imprecise, but by writing everything down, the figures don't lie, it's there in black and white to see.

Proponents claim it works because writing everything down makes you accountable and that changes behavior.

Sound familiar?

Tracking and recording your spending really does change your spending patterns and is why I continue to do it even as my income increases.

Automating your Budget

You're also more likely to stick to your budget the less you have to do which is why automation can work brilliantly.

The more that you can automate your budget the more it'll free up time for other things.

Regular bills are usually the easiest things to automate, especially if they are fixed like the monthly internet bill.

I also like the idea of automating your savings for those on fixed incomes.

Firstly, for automation to work, you need to have money in your account, so if you're the type of person who regularly overdraws, then automation is not for you.

I recommend keeping a minimum balance of a few hundred (or more) to make sure you're always covered if, by chance, you forget a bill is due and go spend that money instead.

I automate my phone, internet, and rent. The rest (generally only utility bills) I pay as they come in.

It's one less thing you have to do.

Setting Up Automation

There are usually two main ways to set up automation.

1. Though the billing provider. There will be instructions on the bottom of your bill or their website on how to do this.

2. Or you can set it up yourself through your bank by creating a recurring monthly (or whatever frequency) payment.

Either option is fine, although it is easier to cancel automatic payments if you've set it up yourself in your own banking app. Sometimes billing providers can be pains in the ankle to try and cancel when you switch from them.

How To Use Your Budget To Get Wealthy

You'll find that after the first month you'll know your spending patterns much better. You'll get a feel for when bills are due, whether it's monthly, yearly, or weekly, and find a rhythm.

Once you've got a handle on that you'll be able to take more control and start to plan for the next stages of becoming wealthy.

Starting a budget was the first step.

The next steps are gaining control over your spending (which you can do now because you know what money you have to work with), pay off debts (if you have them), start a strong savings plan (for the fun stuff), and finally, to invest and have your money work for you.

This isn't a quick fix. Becoming wealthy does take time. But that time is going to pass anyway, so you might as well make plans for your future self so that when you get there you'll thank your past self.

And knowing that there is a better financial future for you if you can stay with it is incredibly motivating.

————

TAKE ACTION

It's time to create your budget.

1. Put On Music.

You don't have to do this step, but music can help it feel more enjoyable.

2. Open your app, spreadsheet, or journal.

Put the month at the top of the page or at the top of a column (depending on what you're using).

3. Create a section for income and add relevant rows (or lines) for all your sources of income.

You might only have one row if you are on a single income, or you might have several if you have several sources of income. Put the total at the bottom.

4. Add another section for expenses and add rows (or lines) for all your expenses.

Group similar items like food or entertainment expenses if it makes sense to do so.

Your expenses rows will usually be longer than your income ones. Total these up.

5. Entering the figures that you know.

An easy way to find most of them is through your banking app. You can easily see what money has come out and what money has gone in to both your main account and your credit card/s.

But don't worry if you don't remember everything yet. You'll add more rows later or consolidate categories as you go. It takes a few months to get a fully functional budget because we invariably always forget something.

I'm still adding rows now as new expenses or sources of income come in.

6. Keep updating it weekly.

I update my budget on a Friday night. Every week I go through what I've spent or earned and update my spreadsheet. It usually only takes ten minutes.

As you continue to update it, you'll see where you are spending your money over time.

7. Automate as much as you can.

To save even more time, set up automation on your finances. Things you can automate include bill paying, transferring money into your savings account, and paying off debts.

STEP TWO - CONTROL YOUR SPENDING

What you'll learn in this section:

- Why most spending is fuelled by marketing and advertising and not real need.
- How to take back control of your spending habits.
- Tips and challenges to cut back on the shopping urge.

Why You Need To Spend Mindfully

THERE IS a principle in economics called the consumption schedule that studies the relationship between income and expenditure.

The basic premise is that in most cases there is an elastic phenomenon whereby a persons average spending increases as they earn more money.

Given a raise or other increase in income, during the first few weeks, the person's spending remains close to the same as it was prior to the change (with a common one-off celebratory spending binge first).

But eventually, their discretionary purchases creep up until they are spending a similar percentage as they were before the increase.

After one year, that person is no better off financially than they were before.

Basically, you earn more money, you buy more expensive stuff to compensate.

But what if you didn't fall into that trap? What if instead you reduced your spending and became more frugal?

Warren Buffett, one of the richest men in the world, lives a modest life considering his wealth. His lifestyle hasn't changed all that much since before he made his billions.

Likewise for many other billionaires. They remain frugal despite their incomes. (Source: https://www.businessinsider.com.au/habits-frugal-billionaires-2017-7).

And it not only makes sense to be frugal for economic reasons, but also for environmental ones. Shopping less means less rubbish from packaging, fewer items to discard, and less overall global wastage.

Of course, you may not even have the luxury of that choice. After creating your budget, you realize that you need to change.

I live simply. I'm not a true minimalist by any means, I

just try to think mindfully about my purchases and save money where I can.

That isn't to say I don't splurge occasionally. I love going on holidays. Nothing beats sipping on a strawberry daiquiri on the deck of a cruise ship at sunset. So I save money in other areas so I can enjoy those moments that have meaning for me and my family.

Take Responsibility For Your Spending

The toughest challenge when it comes to reducing your spending patterns is not the actual cutting spending part. It goes deeper than that. We have ingrained in our unconscious, patterns that go back years.

If you are used to a certain way of living it's hard to justify what many people feel is moving backward instead of forward. Cutting back is not what most people want to do.

We have marketing, friends, neighbors who perpetuate the idea we have of ourselves which includes the type of clothes we wear, the place we live, the things we like.

There is a mentality that we deserve something special if we've had a hard day. We need to take back control and banish that entitlement.

"I deserve it. I had a stressful day. #yolo."

We justify a lot of our purchases. Deep down we know we can't afford all of the things that we buy, but we tell ourselves that we need whatever item it is because of what we have to put up with day to day. Work, kids, the rude person on the freeway.

It's a false economy of course. Because in reality, the stuff we buy doesn't solve whatever stress or unhappiness we have. The shopping high we get when we unbox our goods doesn't last longer than a few hours. It doesn't solve anything long term.

Sure, it feels good in the moment. There is a sense of power and satisfaction owning the new thing. But that feeling fades and by the next week we crave that feeling again and the pattern repeats. Over and over.

"I deserve it," is killing us financially.

So take back responsibility and stop believing that you deserve a shopping reward for your bad day. A better alternative would be to de-stress, whether that's with a warm bath, asking your partner for a back rub, or catching up with friends and having a great laugh.

Those things will make you feel better, and you won't need to spend money to get that high. They say the best things in life are free. Maybe there's some truth to that.

———

KEY TAKEAWAY

Many of us have a spending problem because we live in a world designed to make us spend money.

We see the way we are "supposed" to live everywhere. Advertising, movies, our own neighborhoods.

It makes spending seem normal and thus many people run into problems when they can't keep up.

Become more mindful of the constant marketing and advertising that try and make us feel unworthy unless we do/have something else.

Spending more won't solve your problems.

If you have a hard day don't think that spending is going to solve the problem. It's much deeper than that. Think proactively about other solutions that will fix your mood.

It's your right and responsibility to take back control. Spending is just a quick fix, not a long term solution.

Tips To Cut Back Overspending

SO IT'S ALL VERY WELL to tell you to cut back your spending like it's simple enough to do so. But, we all know that isn't true.

We live in a culture full of marketing and advertising, and even those with the strongest willpower can succumb to wanting the next shiny thing.

We see celebrities wearing expensive designer clothing, or YouTube creators showing how to use the latest lash-lengthening mascara.

The temptation to improve our lives, keep up with our neighbors, do what's expected, is overwhelming.

It's easier to switch our focus and not fight our inclination to want things, but to want the right things.

This chapter will go over some ways that you can cut back on your overspending.

Embrace Becoming More Frugal

Becoming more frugal doesn't mean you have to go without, it simply means that you are making more mindful choices about your spending and choosing where your money goes.

It can also mean that you find less expensive alternatives to your favorite things which can be a fun adventure in itself.

Put simply, becoming more frugal is one of the biggest hacks you can make to your budget to cut back your spending.

So how do you become more frugal?

I think the easiest place to start is at the grocery store. Try and find alternatives to your favorite products. Not everything is going to taste the same, and some brands may not work, but more than half the time you can find some excellent less expensive alternatives to your favorite items just by making a few shopping list tweaks.

Another way to cut back at the grocery store is to avoid buying pre-cut fruits and vegetables. We live in a world of convenience, but buying pre-cut carrots sticks can sometimes cost nearly three times more than buying full carrots and cutting them up yourself.

Also look for ways to cut back on cleaning products. Good old water with a splash of dish soap in a spray bottle can work just as good as specialty cleaners.

Making frugal changes can really have a big impact on your spending and it doesn't take a lot of time.

No-Spend Periods

Every year I try to do a No-Spend Month.

It's exactly what it sounds like. No spending any extra money, apart from the necessities, for a whole month.

The first time I tried it, around seven years ago, it was very successful. I managed to save a cool two grand. That was helped by decluttering and selling some of those unwanted goods on eBay.

I've never managed to save as much in subsequent years (although I was never as motivated as that first time either), but it taught me a lot about my spending habits.

There are so many things that we buy almost unconsciously on a daily or weekly basis. Before that first no-spend month I wouldn't think twice about throwing a few extra items into my shopping cart.

Does my kid want a cheap five-dollar toy from the department store? Sure, add it to the basket. Oh, and that lipstick is on sale. I have a shade similar, but this one looks so creamy. And so on.

I'd justify my purchases because each item was never expensive.

I learned that it's not the expensive things that make you poor, it's the little things over and over. Death by a million paper cuts.

We overspend on things we don't really need, and that realization was never more obvious during my first no-spend month.

Of course, you don't need to do a full month if that seems too intimidating. You could do a week. Or something I'm considering for next year is doing twelve no-spend weekends. One in every month of the year.

I encourage you to try doing one yourself. You'll learn a lot about your spending habits.

The Twenty-Four Hour Rule

To help curb impulse buying you can implement what's called the twenty-four hour rule.

If you see something while you're out shopping or online you stop yourself from throwing that item into the cart. For now.

If you give yourself an imposed time delay on a purchase, chances are that you might not want that item after the twenty-four hours have passed.

If, after the twenty-four hours have passed you still want it, and it fits within your spending budget, then go ahead. However, if you've changed your mind (which I do more often than buying the item) you know it wasn't something you truly needed or desired after all and you save yourself the cash for something better in the future.

This rule can drastically slash your spending and you won't feel like you're denying yourself because if you still really want it after the time limit, you allow yourself to get it.

Calculate the Purchase Cost By Number of Hours Worked

Another good way of curbing spending is to view the

item you want, not by the price it costs but by how many hours it would take you to afford it.

Do you know your hourly wage? You can work it out by dividing your paycheck by the number of hours worked.

So, let's say you make $10 an hour.

If you decide you want a new pair of shoes that cost $80, then you'd need to work eight hours to afford it.

Now ask yourself if those shoes are really worth working eight hours to get.

Unsubscribe from One Shopping Email Per Week

If you've ever shopped anywhere online, you know that from there on, you'll be bombarded with offer after offer from that store.

Marketing emails are relentless. And oh so tempting.

My advice is every day, unsubscribe to one email. It's too overwhelming to try and do it all at once, but one a day is manageable.

Can't bear to unsubscribe from some retailers? Send them to the spam folder instead. That way you won't see them every day but you can choose to actively look for those emails and offers when you're ready to purchase something.

Don't be afraid that you'll miss that one super offer. Those offers come up regularly, and if you're a fan of the store you'll know when the best sales period is already.

Avoid Sales, Unless You Need Something

A sale is not a deal unless you need the item.

Have you ever been in a store and saw something that you weren't looking for and didn't really need but it was such a good deal that you bought it anyway.

Yeah, I think we've all been there.

Next time this happens I want you to ask yourself whether you're attracted to the item or the discount.

Often we get so caught up in the amazing discount (*look it's eighty percent off*), that we don't stop to think whether we actually want the item.

Or we rationalize that we could use it anyway and talk ourselves into it. It's such a good deal that you simply must use it.

Then you get it home and make yourself use it to justify the purchase thereby solidifying in your mind that you did the right thing, even if you would have been perfectly happy without it in your life.

Now there is nothing wrong with a good sale. I like sales, and I like buying things at a discount. But make your shopping trips intentional and planned rather than impulse purchases based solely on price discounts. It can help save on those extra cash bleeds.

Know the sales cycles. Many shops often have sales at the end of the year after Christmas, mid-year, and Black Friday.

Plan your purchases and shop the sales with purpose, rather than simply buy because it looks like a good deal.

Cut These Things From Your Spending

There are things that you could easily cut and do yourself or for which you can find cheaper alternatives. Items that could save you a ton if you cut them from your spending.

Here are some of my favorite things to cut out:

Gym membership

The first thing to look at is if you have a gym member-ship. There are plenty of workouts on YouTube that you can do at home for free. All you usually need is a yoga mat. Or you can go for a walk or run outside.

If it's the equipment that you need, then try and find a smaller gym that doesn't offer classes and is equipment only, or invest in a few weights for home.

If you need instructional guidance, it can be cheaper to hire a personal trainer for a one-time-only training session and ask for a personal work-out plan you can do at home. Many trainers will offer this for an extra fee and this can work out much cheaper than a yearly gym membership.

Bottled water

Get yourself a good reusable water bottle and water filter that you can fill at home. Not only will it save you money, you'll be helping the environment.

Services you can do yourself

If you can do something yourself, you should. Garden-ing, cleaning your house, small DIY jobs. You'd be surprised what you can learn to do from YouTube videos. Obviously, you don't want to attempt anything that requires specialized skills, but most simple DIYs and services are easily done yourself.

Be Your Own Chef and Cook at Home

You can cut spending dramatically by learning how to cook. Buying ready-made meals and take out means that you are not only purchasing that food, but you're paying for the cost of someone else to make it.

Buying the ingredients yourself and recreating your favorite meals will not only work out cheaper, it can also be healthier.

The best way to tackle the supermarket is with a list. Make a rough meal plan of what you'd like to cook that week and a list of ingredients you'll need and stick to the list as much as you can.

When creating your menu, try and incorporate one or two meat-free meals per week. There are many delicious vegetable-based meals that you and your family will love. My family likes macaroni and cheese, veggie pizza (pizza with mushrooms, capsicum, onion, and cheese), and tacos with beans and salad.

Think about using ingredients for more than one meal.

We like to have a roast chicken with salad one night, then use the leftover chicken in a butter chicken recipe the following night.

You don't need to make everything from scratch if you don't have the time. You can buy pizza bases (or use pita bread instead), premade spaghetti sauce, and cake bases that you can ice and decorate yourself.

If you get the kids involved you can make it a fun family event too, and give them skills for later in life.

This is not just for dinner. Packing your own lunches and bringing your own drinks to work or school can save money too.

Invest in a Good Coffee Machine

If you're a coffee drinker like I am, then you'll know that buying a delicious barista made coffee every morning can get expensive very fast. Here in Australia, it's not unusual to spend five to six dollars for one cup of the delicious stuff. Some of the specialty coffees can even run up to eight or nine dollars. Yikes!

But, if you don't want to give up your morning coffee (I didn't), there are great alternatives.

For me, I wasn't about to start drinking instant coffee so

the solution came in the form of a gift of a coffee machine and matching milk frother. It makes the most delicious coffee and I can make a latte for under fifty cents.

While I'll never say that it's as wonderful as a coffee from a good barista, it's a pretty good alternative and one I'm super happy with. It satisfies my craving for my cup of joe, and it saves me money.

Another thing to invest in that won't cost you much is a reusable coffee mug with a lid.

If you take your coffee with you, then you'll need one of these to carry your freshly brewed brew on your travels.

Pack Your Snacks

You all know that packing your lunch for work every day will cut your spending. However, it's not always practical to do so every day. (I do suggest trying though. Start with packing your lunch one day a week, then if that works, twice a week and so on).

But if you're just not into it at all, and prefer to keep buying your lunch (and looking for cheaper options, right?), then consider packing snacks and drinks instead.

You can put together snack packs with fruit, nuts,

cheese, (whatever you like to snack on) and bring that with you. It'll save you from heading to the vending machine and buying a candy bar.

Another way is to bring in your own bottle of water, or if you need your daily orange juice, buying it from the grocery store and bringing it to work with you instead of ducking out and paying twice as much at the corner vendor.

Packing snacks works great for families too. If you've ever been somewhere where the kids complain of being hungry, you can hand over a pre-packed box of snacks to keep them satiated so you don't have to make a detour through the next drive-through window. Healthier and better for the bottom line.

Like Socialising? Embrace the Dinner Party

It seems more fashionable today to eat out at a restaurant with friends than stay at home. And if eating out is your bag, then I've got another tip coming up next.

But why not embrace having dinner parties again? You don't need to call it that if you think it sounds old-fashioned. Call it hanging out or getting together—whatever your friends will go for.

But having dinner parties at your house is a great way to catch up with friends without blowing the budget.

As a bonus, the guest will usually bring the wine, so all you have to do is cook the meal (which if you've embraced cooking from home has become a skill you're mastering anyway).

Make a menu plan based on recipes that everyone will enjoy and decorate the table simply but attractively. Light some candles for ambiance and find a good playlist on Spotify.

No need to worry about making too much noise and annoying other guests, and you can stay as late as you want (and drink as much wine as you want since you won't have to drive home if it's at your house).

The only con is the cleaning up afterward. But that's what dishwashers were invented for, right?

Eating Out Hack

If you must eat out then get the food to go. Find a nice location to eat it such as someone's house, at a picnic spot, or by a river. You get the idea.

Take out is often less expensive than eating in for the

same food. And even if the menu prices are the same, you won't be charged the extras such as drinks, desserts, and other things that add up fast and make your bill higher than you planned.

Look for Dupes of your Favorite Products

If you have a favorite product or brand, there is a very good chance that there is a duplicate product out there for much less money.

While this won't work for every product, it's worth doing some research to see if there is something similar on the market. It could be similar by accident or by design.

Sometimes the dupes can even turn out better than the original. In the case of beauty products, for example, there are many dupes that are just as good, if not better than their more expensive products.

That's not the case for everything though, and it pays to read reviews and do a bit of Googling to see if the dupe will work as a substitute or if it'll be a waste of money.

But for many things I've found wonderful alternatives that I've gone on to love more than the original.

It's worth your time and money to investigate.

Cut Back on the Booze

If you regularly go out socializing you know that it can get pretty expensive. Drinks, food, club entry, etc. can add up fast.

But if socializing is your thing and you have no intention of giving it up, but still want to save some money, this tip will not only save your wallet, it'll keep you from getting drunk too quickly.

Alternate every alcoholic drink with a non-alcoholic drink. So if scotch and Coke is your thing, every second drink you'd just have a plain Coke. Scotch and Coke, plain Coke, scotch and Coke, plain Coke and so on.

Often your friends won't notice that you're not drinking with them, but feel free to let them in on the secret if they're looking to save money as well.

Non-alcoholic drinks can be around fifty to sixty percent cheaper than alcoholic drinks. You can even choose plain water as your alternate drink and save even more as it's often offered free. The advantage of this is that you stay hydrated (and avoid the potential of a hangover).

Or you could just give up alcohol every second weekend, or do a dry July where you don't drink alcohol at all for that month. Not only will your health improve you'll save loads.

Keep Clothing Simple

It can be expensive keeping up with the latest trends in fashion, especially when they seem to change so frequently.

But it doesn't have to be if you buy the right clothing.

Make it your mission to purchase simple cuts and basic clothing that will go with everything.

Very trendy or highly patterned items will go out style much faster than block colored and plain items. A good white T-shirt, for example, can be worn over and over and dressed up or down depending on what you pair it with.

I prefer a neutral wardrobe in whites, greys, blues, and blacks, as these can be timeless. If I want color, it's usually something simple like an accessory or T-shirt I can put under things.

If you're into color, try to keep patterns to a minimum

and buy block colors and bright separates that you can mix and match.

Look for items with good fabric and flattering cuts for your body shape.

Then you can accessorize the items with highly trendy jewelry or scarfs to bring it up to the moment.

Even changing your makeup and hairstyle will make an outfit look different.

By keeping your wardrobe to good basics that fit you well and flatter your shape, you'll save money in the long run and always have something to wear that looks good on you.

Get a Hobby

If you're not going out as much to save money you're going to want something to do. There is only so much Netflix you can binge on before you start craving to do something else.

It used to be that everyone had a hobby. Cooking, collecting, making things. That seems lost now.

So find yourself a hobby.

While some hobbies like photography can get expensive, there are ways to do whatever you're interested in on a budget.

If photography *is* your thing, then start with your smartphone. The camera's on these are amazing and all you need to do is experiment with lighting and angles to get amazing pictures. Adding different filters can bring your photos to another level.

If you're a book reader then either get an ebook subscription so you can read as much as you like or join a library.

Like cooking? Then make it your mission to create delicious budget-friendly meals.

There are so many hobbies that you can start that will not only inspire you and make you feel more fulfilled, they can save you money because you're investing your time doing them rather than spending it at the shopping mall.

START BECOMING mindful about your spending. Marketing and advertising have become so ubiquitous that we are blind to the underlying purpose of those ads which is to part us from our money for stuff that we often don't need.

Is it really making us happy? Or is it making us stressed and scared that we can't really afford all the things that clutter our houses?

Spending is the second step to gaining control of your finances and building long-term wealth.

There is a tremendous feeling of power once you gain control over what you buy. You'll feel liberated that you're no longer a slave to the marketing messages that tell us that if we had the next shiny thing that our lives will be better.

True happiness and joy come from friends, family, and a sense of accomplishment and purpose in life. It doesn't come from mindless spending.

Yet we still need things so we continue to spend money.

It's a vicious cycle.

But gaining control over spending isn't difficult. It just takes a shift in mindset and taking back that power.

There will still be things you want, and that's okay. It's

normal. But you'll be able to prioritize those things that are important with those that you don't.

———

TAKE ACTION

Start a list of all tweaks and hacks to your lifestyle that will result in spending less money.

Things you can try include:

- Look for cheaper alternatives (or dupes) of your favorite products.
- Try a no-spend month, or week, or weekend. It's a good way to save money and take notice of your spending habits.
- Give yourself a time-limit for impulse purchases. Twenty-four hours is a good time frame.
- Work out your hourly rate and think of your purchases in terms of hours worked, rather than the purchase cost.
- Unsubscribe from shopping emails.
- Avoid sales (unless you need something).

- Cut expensive unnecessary items from your budget.
- Make your own food (and coffee).
- Hack socializing with friends by not drinking as much or not eating out as often (choose home parties or midnight picnics instead).
- Wear simple timeless clothing.

STEP THREE - PAY DOWN DEBTS

What you'll learn in this section:

- Why you need to acknowledge what you owe.
- How to make a plan to pay it down.
- Whether you should keep your credit cards after you pay them off.
- Tips and ideas to make paying off debt fun and motivating.
- What to do if if you are still struggling.

Figure Out How Much You Owe

THIS SECTION WILL GO over the steps you need to take to get rid of that weight around your neck—your debts, by figuring out how much you owe and then making a plan to pay it off.

Getting out of debt is the third step in my five steps to wealth. The first being starting a budget, the second gaining control over your spending, the third getting out of debt, the fourth saving, and the fifth investing.

For that reason, you might think that getting out of debt is more important than saving.

In the majority of cases that is true, which is why it's in Step Three and saving is in Step Four, however, the exception is for your yearly expenses fund and emergency fund, which I'll take about in the chapter on What To Save For First in the Savings section.

But apart from those two things, debt does come before saving.

Let's get started.

It's Time to Get Real and Determine How Much Debt You Have

The first step is to actually acknowledge how much debt you have. You can't be an ostrich with your head in the sand if you are going to change things. You need to get real.

But because you're reading this book, I'm guessing you've already committed to that and are willing to follow whatever steps it'll take to pay your debt off.

So face your fear and work out how much debt you have.

Decide What Method You Want To Use to Record All Your Debts.

It's helpful to use the same method to record your debts as you use for your budget.

I personally prefer a spreadsheet because I like to make columns and watch the numbers decrease over time.

Plus you can sort columns by highest interest rate, or lowest balance. You can also make graphs of your progress with a spreadsheet program, which I'll admit is unnecessary, but they look pretty and if you're a visual person, can sometimes help to motivate you.

But like with your budget, you can also use a paper planner or journal if you like to write things down. There are also phone apps that will help you budget and pay off debts too.

Don't overthink it. Use whichever method you prefer, one that is preferably the same as your budget so you can keep everything together, and get on with it.

Write Down All of Your Debts

The next step is to make a list of every debt you have. Whether that's credit cards, personal loans, car loans, your mortgage, etc. Everything that you owe money on.

You might wonder why I'm including your mortgage.

While your mortgage isn't the top priority when it comes to paying down what you owe because the interest rate is usually low and the amount borrowed high, it's still a good idea to keep a record of how it's progressing. And there are plenty of people who want to tackle their mortgages once the rest of their debts are paid off and are now completely debt-free. It's a good goal.

You want to also include in this section, how much money you owe for each of those debts, what the minimum payment is, and what the interest rate is.

You should be able to find out the interest rate and minimum payment on your statements. Your minimum payment will change over time as your debt gets smaller.

Once you've done that, total it up to find out your debt figure.

Phew. The scariest part is over. Now you can fix this.

Displaying your debt somewhere visual

There are some people who feel motivated to display how much they owe somewhere where they can see it every day because it keeps it at the forefront of their focus.

While it's true that writing out your goals and putting them somewhere visual, like a vision board, will give you a higher chance of achieving those goals, I'm not sure I'd want how much I owe on display where anyone might see it.

If the visual reminder does motivate you, then I suggest that instead of a vision board, that you place your debt figure somewhere private where you could still see it every day, but no one else could pry.

Personally, I think it's fine just to keep it in your budget and keep that private.

————

TAKE ACTION

1. Write down a list of all your debts.

This can be in your spreadsheet program, journal, or app that you use for your budget. List them in a new section. Add a row for each debt.

2. Total them up to get your debt number.

It might seem scary now, but in a year's time when you look back, it'll be much smaller and you'll celebrate how far you've come.

How Do You Pay It Off?

HIGHEST INTEREST RATE VS LOWEST BALANCE

YOU'VE ACCOMPLISHED the first step to getting rid of your debt and that's by acknowledging how much you have.

I believe that knowing the truth is the best way to tackle any problem.

The next step is to make a plan on how to start paying it off.

Not having a plan is going to make this more difficult because you'll never have a clear idea of what money you have to use. You've probably already figured that out.

So where do you start?

There are two general strategies to pay down your debts that most people choose.

Pay the Highest Interest Rate

The first is the method of paying the debt with the highest interest rate first, and once that's paid off, moving to the next highest interest rate and so on.

The reasoning behind this method is that by eliminating the highest interest rate first, over time you'll be paying less interest to the banks and be able to get ahead faster.

The less interest that you have to pay to the bank, the better your financial position will be in a shorter amount of time.

Pay the Lowest Balance

The second strategy is instead of paying the highest interest rates, you pay the lowest balance debts first. This strategy is often called the *Debt Snowball Method* made popular by finance author Dave Ramsey.

The reasoning for this method is that with each debt being crossed off your list, it provides motivation to keep going. It's easier and faster to pay off lower balances than higher ones, so you'll have a sense of accomplishment.

You will pay slightly more in interest with this second method, but the upside is that it's more motivating. Once you've paid off that first debt, it can improve your confidence levels knowing that it's possible to be debt-free one day.

OUT OF THE TWO METHODS, I prefer the second method. Having a lot of debt can be overwhelming so paying off the smallest balances first, and crossing them right off your list, can provide confidence over your finances on which you can't put a price (yep, I meant that pun).

How Much Money Do You Have to Pay Off Your Debts?

The amount of money allocated to paying off your debts is going to be different for everyone. It depends on what your income and expenses are.

The only way to know is to have a budget and you've already accomplished that in Step One.

I suggest paying the most money you can on your debts.

But that doesn't mean going without anything else and becoming a miserly bore. All budgets need some discretionary money for small purchases. If you tighten things too much it can suck all the joy out of life. That's not the goal.

Your discretionary purchases should be inexpensive and planned. Budget for a set amount that you can afford and stick to that amount.

Oh, and it goes without saying (which is why I'm saying it), if any spending contributes to more debt, it's a no. The goal is to pay off your debt, not add to it.

How Much to Allocate On Each Debt

Whether you choose the debt snowball method or paying the highest interest rate first, it's time to allocate your payments across all your debts.

I'll use these example figures:

We'll say you have five debts.

- Mortgage, Owe $419,000, minimum payment $2,500 a month, 3.75 percent p.a. interest
- Car Loan, Owe $17,000, minimum payment $300 month, 8 percent interest
- Credit Card One, Owe $567, minimum payment $10, 14 percent interest

- Store Card, Owe $1,360, minimum payment $40, 18 percent interest
- Credit Card Two, Owe $4,293, minimum payment $90, 15 percent interest

Using the Debt Snowball Method, you would off pay Credit Card One first, paying the minimum on the rest. Then when that's paid off in full, you would start working on the Store Card because it has the next lowest balance, and so on.

However, using the highest interest payment method, you would choose to pay the Store Card first because it's got the highest interest rate of eighteen percent, followed by Credit Card Two, which has a fifteen percent rate.

While paying the most on the first debt and the minimum on the rest is the most common way to pay down using both these methods, there is another way that's growing in popularity called the Stagger Method.

Let's look at whether staggering your payments is better than paying the most on the first debt and the minimum on the rest.

The Stagger Method

The stagger method is a variation on how you allocate the money you pay on each debt.

You still allocate the highest portion of your funds to the lowest balance debt (or highest interest rate if you prefer that method) and then stagger the amounts for the rest rather than just put the minimum.

Let's say that after you pay your mortgage at $2,500 a month, you have $1,000 a month to pay the rest of your debts.

Using the example debts above, you might choose to stagger your payments like this:

- Credit Card One: $400 (the most)
- Store Card: $200
- Credit Card Two: $100
- Car Loan: $300 (minimum payment)

You're still paying the most to the main debt that you're concentrating on, but above the minimum payments for the rest (except for the car payment).

But at the end of the month, you would still have all four debts.

Instead, the more common way of paying the most on

your main debt and the minimum on the rest would look like this:

- Credit Card One: $570 (the most)
- Store Card: $40 (minimum payment)
- Credit Card Two: $90 (minimum payment)
- Car Loan: $300 (minimum payment)

Except you only needed $567 for your first debt so, bam, that debt is paid and gone. Yay!

Now you move onto the Store Card and continue the process until you're done with that and eventually eliminate all of those debts one by one.

I prefer this way rather than the stagger method for precisely the reason the Debt Snowball Method works. It eliminates the number of debts you have faster.

Paying the most on one debt and the minimum on the rest is going to allow you to see real progress each time you get rid of a debt, which is incredibly motivating. Never pay the minimum on *all* your debts. Always have one you are working on getting rid of.

Should You Keep Your Credit Cards After You Pay them Off?

I do believe we need some form of credit card in our current world. While it would be ideal to live a cash-only lifestyle, the reality is it's difficult to do so nowadays.

Some people get by with having a debit card rather than a credit card, and if you have a spending problem that's a good option.

But if you've got your spending under control (by creating a budget and a plan), then I don't see credit cards as the enemy, just a tool.

Should you keep all of them, though?

According to the website ValuePenguin (https://www.valuepenguin.com/average-number-credit-cards-per-person), the average number of credit cards that people had in 2017 was 2.35 with an outstanding balance of $5,551.

Having two to three credit cards (with the stats skewing closer to two) is the norm.

While you only need to have one credit card in most cases, I see nothing wrong with having a backup card if, as we've established, you don't have a spending problem.

However, I don't mean having a backup card in case you

get to the limit of the first and you need to do more shopping, but rather a backup in case the first gets lost or stolen.

Having access to a second line of credit in such an emergency can offer peace of mind until the bank sorts out replacing the first one.

Usually, it'll take a week or more to get the first restored which can be a hassle while you're waiting, so having that extra card just makes life easier.

I do recommend only *using* one card at a time though. Not both. Leave the second card at home and only dig it out in an emergency.

Choose a maximum of two cards and get rid of the rest.

Which Credit Card to Choose?

The card you decide to use as your main credit card will depend on what's important to you.

The factors to consider are the interest rate, fees, whether the card has perks or rewards, and if it's a card that's widely accepted around your country and other countries if you travel.

If you can't pay off your card in full every month, then

choosing a low-interest rate makes more sense. If you do pay it off and never carry any debt, then one of the other factors, like a free travel insurance perk, might be more appealing.

Just make sure you read about the other fees on your chosen card. Additional fees on credit cards are often one thing that people don't look into until they are slugged with a $25 charge once a year that they weren't expecting just for the privilege (?!) of having it.

What About Debit Cards Rather Than Credit Cards?

There has been a growing trend over the past few years to use debit cards rather than credit cards.

A debit card works in the same manner as a credit card (in that you can use it to buy things rather than using cash), but instead of buying on credit, you're buying with your own money.

There are two ways this happens.

One is a debit card that is linked to your main bank account and it pulls the funds from there, and the second is a debit card where you put money into it in order to use it.

There are pros and cons to both.

A debit card that is linked to your bank account is useful because you don't have to do anything else, but you always need to be sure that you have the money in your account otherwise you might accidentally overdraw with it.

A debit card that you put money on up front is more secure (because it's not linked to your account), but means that if you lose it, you've lost all the money on it. Sometimes it's also hard to spend every cent you put on and small balances are left on the card.

Debit cards have no interest payments like a credit card (because you're not borrowing money), but sometimes there are fees associated with them, of which you need to be aware.

Make sure you find out if there are any additional fees associated with your card.

While I prefer the regular old credit card, I do think debit cards are a great alternative for many. They provide all the benefits of a credit card without the interest rates.

TAKE ACTION

1. Decide which method of paying off your debt you prefer.

Choose either the Highest Interest Rate First Method or the Debt Snowball Method.

2. Sort your debts according to your chosen method.

If that's the highest interest rate first, that debt goes at the top and will be your main focus. If it's the lowest balance put that at the top.

3. Each month (or period you get paid) start paying down your debt.

You want to start your payment plan based on how often you get paid. If you get paid monthly, pay your debts monthly. Don't wait to the due dates, pay them as soon as you get paid so that money is accounted for.

Based on what you determined you could afford to pay, put the most on your main debt, and the minimum payment on the rest.

4. Once you've paid off your credit card/s, decide whether you're going to keep using it

(responsibly), or if you want to switch to a debit card instead.

They both have advantages and disadvantages. Weigh up which option would work best in your circumstance.

Credit cards are useful tools if used correctly and paid off in full each month. But if the allocated credit is too tempting, switch to a debit card instead.

Make Paying Off Debt Fun

TIPS TO MOTIVATE AND GAMIFY THE DEBT PROCESS

THERE ARE lots of different ways to pay off your debts. In the last chapter, I went through the steps of figuring out how much you owe, and then working out which method of paying it off that you preferred.

All important and helpful information, but not exactly inspiring. Right?

So now it's time to go deeper and talk about ways not only to find extra money to pay off that debt faster but also make it super motivating and fun too.

Er, fun? Stay with me. It's time we played a game.

Gamify Paying Off Your Debts

Have you ever played a game, perhaps on your phone, or your kid's console, that you became obsessed with?

You couldn't put down the controller, or stop repeating a certain level because if you just got to the next step, you'd gain powers or points or gems or ... it didn't matter what it was. All that mattered was that you did it. That you passed the level.

Those games are addictive because with each achievement your brain releases a small amount of dopamine. Dopamine is a pleasure chemical that's wicked powerful for increasing motivation.

It can also lead you to do things that aren't so good for you too, like gambling or drugs. It's a hard high to break.

Numerous studies say that we can use this chemical to our benefit, rather than our detriment. We can replace the bad habits with another that gives equal pleasure.

That's where gamification theory comes in. It's turning things we want to do in real life into a game. Creating levels and goals for reaching milestones where the theory goes, we are rewarded not only with "points" but also that same dopamine rush.

Gamify Your Finances

Paid $100 off your credit card? Bam! You just reached the next level, my friend.

We do this already in some capacity. Completed a gym workout? Go treat yourself to a new T-shirt. Happy chemical rush (and a new top).

The science still is unclear whether gamification can completely change your motivation the same way it seems to with computer games. Some studies say it does, others say it has no noticeable effect. (*Source: https://journals.uair.arizona.edu/index.php/itet/article/view/18661/18410*)

But what is agreed is that giving yourself rewards *is* something we already do and it's worth using to create new healthier habits.

Like paying off unwanted debts.

Using a Points System

The points system is a very simple version of gamification. The basic premise is that you get one point for every dollar that you pay off your debt, and you lose a point if you add to the debt.

Your goal is to reach certain points levels.

One hundred points and you can treat yourself to a small inexpensive (or free) reward. Something like a luxurious bubble bath, or renting the $0.99 movie of the week from iTunes (every so often they have one that's decent).

One thousand points and you spend the day at the beach with your family/friends, or visit an art gallery, or watch a new band at the local hangout.

The point rewards that you choose should be things that are motivating and meaningful to you.

Make a list of everything you've always wanted to do but never have time for. Things that would make you happy and feel fulfilled. They *can* cost small amounts, but nothing that would create more debt.

Allocate different points levels to each of those rewards.

Bingo! You've just created your first game to paying off your debt. Go accumulate those points. The game starts now.

Don't Break the Chain

Don't Break the Chain is a method that was made famous by comedian Jerry Seinfeld. In his version, he would make sure he wrote something, a new joke or observation, every single day. Something that he might be able to use in his stand up routines.

Every single day he'd mark his calendar on the days he completed his task. His goal: never miss a day, don't break the chain.

You can apply the same principle to your own life for anything you like, including paying off your debts.

But instead of writing something every day, you would change your chain to doing something every week toward becoming debt-free.

Every single week you need to do something extra, on top of what you're already doing, that will take you a step closer to becoming debt free.

That could be adding additional money to one of your credit cards. Selling something you own to use that money as an extra loan payment. Taking up a side hustle for the sole purpose of using that income to pay off that debt even faster. Or even as simple as choosing not to buy something that you really want until you can afford it in the future.

Every single week you make a commitment to doing one extra thing toward becoming debt free.

Create a weekly calendar. Those weeks will add up fast and you'll see real progress. Mark each week that you do something to help you reach your goal.

And don't break the chain.

Reward Yourself For Reaching Milestones

Okay, so I've convinced you that making paying off debt fun, and it will help you to become more motivated.

Points and goals and challenges are all great, but what sort of rewards are you going to give yourself?

Different rewards work for different people, so you'll need to brainstorm what kinds of rewards will work for you.

I personally prefer experience type rewards over things. I find memories and enjoying life can be more motivating than objects. You might be the same or different.

Here are some ideas to get you started:

- Spend the night binge-watching your favorite Netflix show complete with wine and popcorn.
- Relax in a bubble bath complete with candles and soft music.
- Make a coffee date with that friend who you

haven't see in months and spend the afternoon catching up on each other's lives.

- Take the kids on a picnic to the closest beach/farm/playground.
- Snuggle in bed with toasted buttery croissants, hot coffee, and a new book.
- Sip cocktails at the edge of a riverbank at sunset.

They can all be done alone or with someone you care about.

———

TAKE ACTION

1. Make games out of paying off your debts.

Gamification has been shown to increase motivation.

2. Create a points system complete with rewards for reaching certain "levels" or amounts of debt paid off.

Make a list of things that you want to do or have when you reach each milestone.

Keep the rewards no or low cost but something you'd want to try and "win".

3. Start a calendar "chain" system.

Each week do something extra to pay off your debt. Mark your calendar if you complete your task so you can see your progress. Don't miss a week.

Quit Creating More Debt

AND WHAT TO DO IF YOU ARE STILL STRUGGLING

THE ROAD to becoming debt-free should be a journey. Sometimes that journey will take a long time, other times it'll be a short stroll around the block. But the destination at the end is sweet and free and something we should all strive for.

You already know how much stress and struggle it is when you have debts and bills piling up. It's not fun. I prefer to live a simpler life, a life where I can live within my means, but still brings joy.

Make a commitment to yourself not to add any more debt to your life. I'm obviously talking about loans and credit cards here, not mortgages. Having a house can provide security that's important to many of you.

It's the bad debts, the ones that eat at your happiness because you spend the night worrying about how you're going to pay for them, that are the killer to your finances.

You've come this far and you've gained control over your spending. You have a budget. You know how to do this now.

From here on it's your goal to not buy anything you can't afford. If you want it that badly, then save for it.

Don't believe in instant gratification, it's too fleeting. Work toward something by saving and earning it. This will give the item much more meaning when you do get it.

Pay Credit Card Purchases the Same Week You Make Them

I use my credit card multiple times a week.

To ensure that I'm never slugged with any interest payments, I make sure to keep my balance at zero.

When I make a purchase, once that transaction comes up on my credit card statement, I transfer the money from my regular account to my credit card. Immediately. Right away. Or at least, that night when I have a few minutes to myself.

Lots and lots of small transfers. I don't wait until I get the end of month statement and do one lump sum payment. I'm proactive about it and start paying the amounts as soon as they appear. A $47.30 charge here, $15.95 there.

Because the transactions always show up within a day or two, it's also a good way of remembering what you purchased.

There were times before I started doing this that I'd wonder what a transaction was because the store name wasn't familiar (sometimes purchases come up under parent company names rather than the store name). If you're constantly doing this, you tend to remember where you spent that $23.85 on Monday.

Check your balance regularly to allow yourself to stay on track of where you are and keep on top of your credit card usage.

Make it your mission to get your card to zero balance and then keep it there by paying for purchases as soon as possible.

No one wants to pay the bank extra money. Interest sucks and keeps you from getting ahead.

Keep Up Those Payments

Keep up the regular payments even if it feels like it's not going anywhere. It is. You just can't see it much in the beginning. Once you see those numbers on your debts get smaller you're making progress, no matter how long it takes.

Eventually, your debt will be gone. You achieve that which you focus on.

Should You Cut Up Your Credit Cards?

I've heard it before. Cut up your cards so you won't be tempted to use them. Freeze them in a chunk of ice, if you still want it after the ice has thawed then it was a legitimate want.

Cutting up credit cards is the adult equivalent of taking a child's toy away when they're being naughty. It doesn't teach us anything, it just makes us resentful.

It can also be detrimental to your credit score.

It might work in the short term, but we live in a world where buying on credit is a reality. If it's that much of a problem for you, then consider a debit card instead.

I won't be cutting up my credit cards.

Used in a responsible manner, credit cards are not the enemy. They can be useful, and in today's world, necessary.

You just need to take the control back. Debt can be managed with education and a solid plan of attack. Not a solid block of ice with your card inside.

Should You Consider a Zero Percent Balance Transfer?

Most banks offer credit cards where you can transfer the balance of your current card without interest for a specific term.

The term usually varies, but most often is for one year.

This can be a great way to give yourself a break from the interest and help pay down the balance on your old card quicker.

However, if you want to use this strategy you need to be aware of some of the catches that come with this offer.

Firstly, the credit card will usually attract a high-interest rate once the term is up. Make sure you check what that interest rate will be before signing up.

Secondly, the zero percent interest only applies to the

balance that you transfer over, not for any extra purchases that you make with the new card.

This strategy can be used successfully, but only if you think that you can pay the full balance within the term that includes the zero percent interest.

If that's not the case, and you want to switch cards because your current card has high interest, a better strategy would be to transfer the balance to a low-interest card instead.

Negotiating a Lower Interest Rate

If you want to keep your current card but you're struggling to get the balance down, it can be a good idea to call your bank to see if they'll be able to offer a lower interest rate.

Before you call, check out their website for their current advertised rates. Banks change their advertised interest rates regularly to attract new customers and it's always worth checking if their credit card interest rates are the same as the one you currently have.

You've got a greater chance of getting an interest rate reduction if the current rates are lower than what you're at now. It also helps if you've been a regular customer of the bank over many years.

It's scary to call, I know, but what's the worst that can happen? They say they can't help, then no big deal.

If they can help and lower your interest rate, even just a few points, then it was worth finding out.

What About a Debt Consolidation Loan?

If your debts are considerable, and even after all your pay down strategies are in place and you're not seeing any progress, you might consider a debt consolidation loan.

Refinancing your debts into the one loan is something that you need to be serious about before going through with. There are risks to it and it isn't the right decision for everyone. I would suggest that it shouldn't be a first choice.

Often there are conditions attached to those loans and they still have high-interest rates. Do your research and find a reputable debt consolidation company or see if your current bank offers the option, and read all the fine print before signing anything.

It's a big decision and only one you should take if you've tried everything else and can see no other option.

Also, before you jump into such a loan, please give more time to paying off your current debts. See where you are after a year. Just in case.

And I know you can do it. You've already taken the beginning steps.

You've got this.

———

KEY TAKEAWAY

Commit to not making any further debt.

Now that you have a plan in place, you need to commit to not making any further debt.

If you use your credit card, make the payments as soon as those transactions show up on your statement. If you can't do this daily, then at least do it weekly.

If your debt is out of control, try and negotiate a lower rate on your card. The worst the bank will say is no and then you're no better or worse than before you asked.

Above all, have confidence that you can do this no matter how long it takes. And if you can't, there are options available to you.

But at least, try for a year and see where you get before going down the other paths. You might surprise yourself!

STEP FOUR - START SAVING

What you'll learn in this section:

- Why you should save.
- How many bank accounts you should have.
- Setting up a savings account and what to look for.
- Making a plan on what things you want to save for.
- Tips to find more money to add to your savings.

Why Save?

IS THERE A MAGIC AMOUNT TO SAVE?

THE NEXT STEP to becoming wealthy is to start saving.

In this section, I'm going to show you how to start saving money, where to put it, and what to save for.

We all know that saving is important, but most people don't place as much importance on it as they should.

I believe the reason for that is that it's just not exciting. Added to that is that we are told so many different amounts of money that we should be saving that it can be confusing.

Are you supposed to save ten percent of your income, twenty percent, more, or less?

I'll answer that question in a moment, but first, let me give you one tip that I think will help with your savings goals.

Always be Saving for Something.

I often find people who say they can't save money, are usually those that don't have a reason to save. They aren't motivated to do so.

But if you find a reason to save, whether it's for something big or something small, you'll be more likely to want to put that money away rather than spend it at the moment.

It's why it's easier to save when you're planning a holiday or a wedding because that goal becomes your motivation to do so. It excites you.

When it comes to saving money, you always want to have at least one thing that you're aiming for.

Always be saving. It could be a house deposit, or a European holiday, or perhaps a new car. And you need to know how much that goal costs in real terms so you know how you're progressing toward it.

What motivates you to save will be different from what

motivates others. All people have different things that motivate them. So whatever you choose has to be something that makes you want to stick to your savings plan.

For me, security is my number one motivation. I save money on the small things so that I can secure money and an income for myself and my family over the long term. I do that by investing in the stock market (which I'll go into later). But that's my thing. Your motivation for saving is likely to differ.

My goals are what make me want to save rather than spend. And your goal should make you want to do the same.

It should be motivating enough so that when you are tempted to buy something you don't need that you're strong enough to say enough. You want the big thing more than the small item right now.

How Much Money Should You Be Saving?

Right up front, I'm going to tell you that there isn't a magic standard percentage or amount that fits everyone.

I know you've heard that you should be saving twenty percent of your income or another standard figure, and

I'll admit that it's an easy answer to give people when they ask.

Many people want a concrete answer and twenty percent allows the amount to vary according to how much income is coming in.

It sounds reasonable. I'll even admit that in my early financial advice days I recommended a percentage of income too.

But the problem with one-size-fits-all answers is that it doesn't take into account the differences in people's lives and circumstances.

Twenty percent is likely too much for someone who is the sole provider of one or more family members or it might be too little for a single person living at home with no expenses.

Saving money should empower people financially, not make them feel they aren't doing it the "right" way.

The amount you should save needs to come back to your unique situation and the only true way to figure out how much you can afford to save is to have a budget.

Yep, the boring old budget again. Like before, it's going

to let you know how much money you have available to save.

That amount should be the money you have left over. If you've allocated all your bills and necessities and given yourself some fun spending money (but not too much), whatever is left over should go into your savings account.

So save as much money as you are able to and you'll reach your financial goals that much sooner.

———

TAKE ACTION

1. Make saving a priority.

Factor it into your budget so you do it every month.

2. What do you want to save for?

You should always be saving for something. What's your thing?

Save for one thing at a time to make it happen faster. Then save for the next thing, and so on.

3. Commit to saving as much of your excess

income as you can while still allowing yourself some discretionary income.

While you still should allocate some of your budget to discretionary spending, you also need to save as much as you can. It's a balancing act to decide how much, but a good rule of thumb is to save as much as your budget will allow without taking the joy out of each month.

Where To Put Your Savings

OKAY, so I've convinced you to save as much as is right for you. Great, but now where are you going to put your money?

You need to find a high-interest savings account that is separate from your everyday transaction account.

That's all you need. Two bank accounts. One for your day-to-day expenses that is easy to access, and one in which you're going to put your savings.

Keep it simple.

When choosing a savings account the main things to look for are:

1. the interest rate,
2. whether the account has any fees associated with it,
3. how easy it is to deposit and withdraw your money, and
4. if it can be linked to your everyday transaction account.

Interest Rates

Generally, online-only savings accounts have the highest yields (interest rates).

Many of them offer two tiers of interest. A standard rate for having money in the account, and a bonus rate. The bonus rate is extra interest on top of the standard rate that you get for meeting certain criteria. Usually that criteria is depositing a set amount of money into the account every month.

Right now, in Australia, the average standard rate for online savings accounts is two percent p.a. up to three percent if you include bonus rates.

Most of the major banks have online accounts, but you'll find the smaller banks such as ING Direct, Citibank,

RAMS, and HSBC will have slightly higher interest rates because they want to attract your business.

Fees

It's rare for any of the online accounts to have monthly or yearly fees (but do check the fine print).

The most common fees associated with these accounts is a charge to withdraw your money from an ATM or over the counter at the bank itself. Not all of them have this but it's worth being aware of it.

Other fee's you need to be aware of is if they charge for having less than a minimum amount in the account. Again, not many of them have this, but it's worth finding out.

Ease of Deposit and Withdrawal

You need to be able to easily add money and withdraw into your savings account as you please. That might be by linking it to your everyday bank account or having convenient access to an ATM or branch (without fees for doing so, as mentioned above).

You will be more likely want to save your cash if it's easy to do so.

Linking to Your Transaction Account

I like savings accounts that are linked to my everyday transaction account so that I can quickly transfer funds between the accounts. You can do that with most online accounts, even if the account isn't with the same bank.

There are generally no fees associated with this and it's just a matter of logging into your savings account (either online or through your bank phone app) and enter the amount you want to transfer.

You can also set up recurring deposits and see your growing balance (and growing interest deposits) which can be incredibly motivating.

That's it.

What About a Savings Account That Has Lots of Different Sub-accounts?

There is a trend right now where you can split your main savings account up into lots of different "sub" accounts. The idea is that you can place different amounts of money into each slice that you've allocated to different saving goals.

So one sub-account might be for saving for a car, another for a holiday, another for Christmas, and so on. The idea is that you can focus on saving for every single thing on your wish-list.

While having such options sounds great in theory, it doesn't work out so well in practice. In my experience, the more accounts that you have, the less you can achieve all those individual goals because you are diluting your savings power.

The motivation that you'll reach your goals becomes smaller because it takes all that much longer to reach just one of them. You've split the pie too much.

I'm not saying that you can't have more than one goal for your savings, everyone always has more than one thing they want in life. But having multiple accounts complicates the goal of saving as easily and effortlessly as possible.

The exception would be if you want to keep your emergency fund and yearly expenses fund separate from the rest of your savings. It isn't necessary though. You can keep them all in the same account.

Have one account and save for what you want one thing at a time. You'll achieve those goals much faster and be able to move onto the next item on your list while enjoying the first thing. Now that's motivating.

You want a savings account that will give you the best return possible. Not one that can slice up your savings into ten different sub-accounts.

What about Term Deposits or Bonds instead of a Savings Account?

Term deposits and government bonds are very popular with people not comfortable with investing, and with good reason, it's a guaranteed return on your money. There is little risk.

The idea is that you lock away your money for a predetermined period and at the end of that term you get back your money, with interest.

Right now, the interest rates for term deposits and government bonds is around 2.5 percent p.a.

As you can see, that's not a lot different from the interest rate for most online savings accounts. Perhaps half a percent higher if you're lucky.

I don't believe that half a percent is worth having your money tied up and inaccessible for six, twelve, or even sixty months.

Keep your money in a savings account that offers a similar

interest rate and that you can access at any time. It's simpler to set up and offers the same security. Term deposits and bonds might be safe, but they're not as convenient.

———

TAKE ACTION

1. Simplify your bank accounts into two main accounts.

- One is your regular everyday transaction account. This account should be easy to access. It's the one that your paycheck and other income will go into.
- The second is a high-interest savings account. This is where you'll save up for all those things you want in the future.

2. Decide on a savings account:

- Whether you prefer the convenience of using the same bank as your regular transaction account, or

- The highest interest rate (even if that's with another bank).

3. Research any fees or bonus interest that the savings account might incur.

Avoid fees where possible, and see if you are eligible for bonus interest. Depositing a set amount is often enough to gain 0.5% to 1% extra which is better in your pocket than the banks.

4. If you haven't already, open your high-interest savings account and start saving.

Research the bank you want to use for your savings account and open an account. Look for a good interest rate, ease of transaction, and no hidden fees.

What To Save For First

THE GENERAL ADVICE is to start saving after you've paid off your debts, and *generally* that would be true.

However, there are two things that you should start saving for first. That is your yearly expenses fund and your emergency fund.

You can't attack your debt, without making sure that you've set up a system so that you're not adding to your credit card later down the line because you can't pay your car registration.

By saving for these either before you start attacking that debt or at the same time, it will prevent you having to get into more debt down the line.

Saving for both your yearly expenses fund and your emergency fund will prevent further debt as you'll be prepared for those future expenses.

Your Yearly Expenses Fund

To start your savings journey off on the right foot, the very first thing that you should save for is your yearly expenses fund.

The yearly expenses fund is for those expenses that come around once per year.

Things like your car insurance, auto registration, or holidays and birthdays. Whatever larger expenses you have that blow the budget every year.

To determine how much to pay into this fund you need to determine what annual expenses you have.

In either your spreadsheet or budget journal, create an extra page (or tab) to list your expenses.

Make sure you include the date that they are due if you know them. Otherwise just make an educated guess. Then arrange them in the approximate date order that they are due.

Add up all those expenses and divide by twelve (if you get paid monthly) or fifty-two (if you get paid weekly).

That's the amount, plus a little extra to be sure, you are going to put into your yearly expenses fund. By doing so you'll have those expenses covered by the time they come around.

Your Emergency Fund

Once your yearly expenses fund is set up, the next thing to save for is your emergency fund.

Your emergency fund is a set amount of money that you've put aside to deal with any financial emergencies that might crop up.

It's so you can use that saved cash instead of having to use your credit card. Sort of like creating your own insurance for what you might need to purchase in a hurry.

How much do you need in your emergency fund?

There is a lot of debate on how much you actually need in your emergency fund. Most people overestimate what they'll actually need.

A good amount to aim for is between five hundred and

two thousand dollars. Small enough to save quickly and large enough to cover most minor emergencies.

Generally, the emergency fund is to pay for things like a new washing machine if your old one breaks, or minor car repairs. Things like that.

It's not for creating a year's worth of income in case you lose your job. There is plenty of time later for that if you feel you need to. This is just for the smaller emergencies, the ones you would have likely put on your credit card to pay for.

It doesn't matter which account you put your emergency fund into. Put it in either your regular account or your savings account. It's up to you. The only importance here is that you can access the money quickly if you need it.

Once you have a yearly expenses fund and an emergency fund set up, you can start to save for the bigger, more exciting fun things.

———

TAKE ACTION

1. Start your yearly expenses fund.

Make a list of all your annual expenses and total it. Divide that number by how often you get paid.

That's how much you'll need to put into your yearly expenses fund each paycheck to cover those costs.

2. Start an emergency fund.

Save up an amount between $500 and $2,000 depending on how much things cost in your area.

This will cover those unexpected small emergencies that crop up.

How To Fast Track Your Savings

SAVINGS CHALLENGES AND MOTIVATION

YOU'VE SET up your savings account. Now it's time to fast track your savings so that you can get to your goals sooner.

Many people believe that it takes too long to save for something so why bother when you can spend today? So let's speed up that savings plan.

This chapter will cover ways you can automate how much you save, give you some fun savings challenges, and provide tips on how to find extra money. All these can help to boost your savings.

You'll reach your savings goals in no time.

Automate Your Savings

An easy way to get your savings rolling is by setting up an automatic transfer from your regular account to your savings account.

This can be set up on the day that you get paid, or any other timeframe that works best for you.

Setting up an auto payment will save you time and it's one less task that you have to think about.

I'm a fan of putting as much of your finances on autopilot as possible. Bills, savings, paying debts etc.

Free up your time and get on with living your life. Isn't that the whole point?

The Steps to Automate your Savings

So how do you do it?

First, decide how much you're going to regularly transfer into your savings account. Choose a figure that slightly lower than what you've budgeted to save.

If you have allocated four hundred dollars a month for savings, then make your auto transfer three hundred dollars a month. You can always add the remainder at the end of the month.

I like having the auto transfer a little less so that I don't have to worry about not having enough in my bank account.

There have been one or two times where an automatic bill payment that I'd forgotten about has been withdrawn and I've gotten close to not having enough in the account when the savings auto-payment came out. (*Now I always have a buffer of at least five hundred dollars in my account and don't let it dip below that*).

Next, you need to determine which day of the week or month that's the best to do the automatic transfer. If you get paid on a specific day, make the auto-payment a day or two after that (again, just to make sure that the funds have gone into your account correctly).

You can set up automatic transfers and payments through your banking app via your phone or computer.

Round-up Features

Another way to automate your savings is to set up a round-up feature based on your spending.

The basic concept of a round-up feature is that it "rounds up" whatever you spend on your credit or debit card to the nearest dollar and places the difference into an account.

So if you spend $6.25 on a purchase it will round up the purchase to $7.00, placing the difference, in this case, seventy-five cents, into a specified account.

There are a few different banking companies coming on board with this, ING in Australia has been advertising it heavily recently. The major banks haven't started this yet although I suspect they will in the future.

Another way to use the round-up feature is with micro investing apps like Acorns. (*It's recently been renamed to Raiz in Australia*).

With this (and similar apps) the difference gets deposited into an Exchange Traded Fund (ETF) rather than a regular savings account. ETF's are my favorite way to get started investing in the stock market and I mention them in the chapter on investing later in this book.

With these apps, you can choose between different ETF's based on your risk threshold.

It isn't free though. In the Raiz app, balances under $5,000 attract a $1.25 fee per month. Over $5,000 and it's 0.275 percent p.a. based on your balance. That's not unreasonable compared to other ETF fees, however.

Acorns in the US have similar fees.

So while you can potentially earn more than a regular savings account, if you have a small balance, those fees can eat away any gains. For that reason, it's only worth using if you can keep a balance over $500.

And another thing is I wouldn't keep more than $10,000 in it. If your balance gets that high, take some out and put it directly into the stock market (or other investment of your choice).

Of course, you can also do this yourself by tracking your spending and putting the extra into your savings account yourself, although that wouldn't be automated.

It's a very similar concept to putting your spare change in a jar each day (if you use cash), and then taking the jar to the bank once it gets full.

All those little increments add up.

Create a Savings Challenge

Do you push yourself harder when there is a challenge involved?

I do and it's the same with many people. It's why gamification (turning everyday tasks into a game with rewards) works so well. I've already talked about this concept when paying off your debts. The same can be applied to saving.

The best savings challenges are the ones that are simple and fun and let you build up fast savings.

There are plenty out there to choose from. I've included some of my favorites below, but if these aren't for you there are plenty more you can try.

Scour Pinterest, blogs, or Facebook groups to find your favorite or try one of these.

Are you up for a challenge?

The 52-Week Savings Challenge

Okay, you've no doubt seen this one before. It's usually the first challenge that comes up when you search for savings challenges. There's a good reason for that. It's simple and it's achievable.

If you don't know, the idea with the 52-week savings challenge is that you start by saving $1 in week one and then each week you increase the amount of money by an extra dollar. So in week two, you save $2. Week three, $3 and so on, right up to week fifty-two, saving $52.

The amounts aren't a lot, but it shows the power of regularly saving even small amounts can add up fast. By the end of the challenge, you would have saved $1,378 over the fifty-two weeks.

You are meant to start the challenge at the start of the year and finish at the end. But in reality, you can start whenever you like. Week one doesn't have to be the first week in January, it can be the first week after your birthday, or next week, or today.

It doesn't matter when you start.

It can also be done in reverse, starting with saving $52 in the first week and then working back to $1 in the last.

I've heard doing it in reverse is easier because you have higher motivation at the beginning of the challenge. Plus if you put your money into a high-interest account, putting the higher amounts first means you'll earn more interest overall due to compound interest.

Here's what the regular 52-week challenge looks like:

- Week 1 - save $1 - balance $1
- Week 2 - save $2 - balance $3
- Week 3 - save $3 - balance $6
- Week 4 - save $4 - balance $10

- Week 5 - save $5 - balance $15
- Week 6 - save $6 - balance $21
- Week 7 - save $7 - balance $28
- Week 8 - save $8 - balance $36
- Week 9 - save $9 - balance $45
- Week 10 - save $10 - balance $55
- Week 11 - save $11 - balance $66
- Week 12 - save $12 - balance $78
- Week 13 - save $13 - balance $91
- Week 14 - save $14 - balance $105
- Week 15 - save $15 - balance $120
- Week 16 - save $16 - balance $136
- Week 17 - save $17 - balance $153
- Week 18 - save $18 - balance $171
- Week 19 - save $19 - balance $190
- Week 20 - save $20 - balance $210
- Week 21 - save $21 - balance $231
- Week 22 - save $22 - balance $253
- Week 23 - save $23 - balance $276
- Week 24 - save $24 - balance $300
- Week 25 - save $25 - balance $325
- Week 26 - save $26 - balance $351
- Week 27 - save $27 - balance $378
- Week 28 - save $28 - balance $406
- Week 29 - save $29 - balance $435
- Week 30 - save $30 - balance $465

- Week 31 - save $31 - balance $496
- Week 32 - save $32 - balance $528
- Week 33 - save $33 - balance $561
- Week 34 - save $34 - balance $595
- Week 35 - save $35 - balance $630
- Week 36 - save $36 - balance $666
- Week 37 - save $37 - balance $703
- Week 38 - save $38 - balance $741
- Week 39 - save $39 - balance $780
- Week 40 - save $40 - balance $820
- Week 41 - save $41 - balance $861
- Week 42 - save $42 - balance $903
- Week 43 - save $43 - balance $946
- Week 44 - save $44 - balance $990
- Week 45 - save $45 - balance $1035
- Week 46 - save $46 - balance $1081
- Week 47 - save $47 - balance $1128
- Week 48 - save $48 - balance $1176
- Week 49 - save $49 - balance $1225
- Week 50 - save $50 - balance $1275
- Week 51 - save $51 - balance $1326
- Week 52 - save $52 - balance $1378

Save Your Fives Challenge

The Save Your Fives money challenge is where every time you get a five-dollar bill you add it to your savings.

It works like this:

Let's say you buy something with cash and hand over a twenty and get a five-dollar bill and some coins as your change.

Sock that five-dollar bill away and keep it safe. You can't spend that fiver now because it's going into your savings.

Do this each and every time you are given a five-dollar bill, either as change, finding it in the street, or whenever you stumble across one.

Five dollars works because it's a smallish amount so it's not so intimidating. But it's also large enough that you'll see a dramatic difference in how much you can put away.

It's entirely possible to do this with your dollar bills (or coins) if you prefer, but doing it with a fiver means your savings will add up much faster.

This challenge does mean that you'll need to commit to using cash rather than your card for smaller purchases though. Otherwise, those five-dollar bills won't come as fast, and that's kind of the point of the whole challenge.

No-Spend Month / Week / Year Challenges

I've talked about how I like doing a no spend month once a year in the spending section of this book (Step Two). It can also be another great way to add some extra quick cash to your savings.

We don't need as much stuff as we buy, and doing a no-spend really brings that mindfulness to our spending habits back into focus (and can help save a lot of money while doing it).

Spending Equals Savings Challenge

The Spending Equals Savings challenge is where you match any discretionary spending you do and put an equal amount into your savings account.

How it works:

Let's say you want to buy a small indulgence, maybe a fancy coffee at a cafe, and it costs four dollars. You can buy it for four dollars, but you also have to match that by putting four dollars into your savings account.

Each time you make *any* discretionary purchase, you match it and put the same amount into your savings.

$10 book = $10 into your savings. $50 drugstore splurge = $50 in your savings. And so on.

Not only is it a good way to build your savings, it's also a good way to keep track of your spending.

Because if you can't afford to put the same dollar amount into your savings account, perhaps you can't afford that item after all.

Adding Lump Sums to Savings

Another good way to boost your savings is to put any lump sums, tax refunds or windfalls that you weren't expecting, into your savings account.

The average tax refund in Australia according to the Australian Tax Office (source: https://www.etax.-com.au/average-tax-refund-sept-12/) is more than $2,300. It's a little more in the USA, with the average taxpayer receiving $2,700.

Let's average that out to $2,500 a year and see what would happen if you saved that amount and placed it into a savings account at two percent p.a. No extra money, just your tax refund.

For the sake of simplicity, I'll use the example of the account only paying interest on the final balance, but most accounts pay interest on the daily balance so your actual return will be slightly higher than I've put here.

- End of Year One: $2,550 (*you put in $2,500 and earned $50 interest over that year*).
- End of Year Five: $13,270 ($12,500 *of your money, $770 interest, over the past five years*).
- Year Ten: $27,922 ($25,000 *of your money, $2,922 interest*).
- Year Twenty Five: $81,677 ($62,500 *of your money, $19,177 interest*).

The longer you leave it in, the higher the amount of interest you'll receive over the lifetime of that account.

I love compound interest.

Purge & Sell

You can fast track your savings and provide a great initial boost by doing a big declutter of your current belongings and selling those items that have worth.

Start room by room so you don't become overwhelmed and pull out everything that you no longer use or want.

Place all of those items somewhere where you can see

them, a floor or table is good. Then see what you have that you could sell.

Bundling is good for similar items like books or DVDs, rather than selling them individually (and you get can get rid of them in one fell swoop). You can list your items on places like eBay, Craigslist, Mercari or Facebook sell and swap groups.

Make sure to factor in postage costs (which the buyer pays) and you can get rid of all your unwanted stuff and make some serious cash, all in one go.

Purge and sell for cash works for large items too. Downsizing to one car instead to two, getting rid of the jetski you only use once a year (it'll be cheaper to hire one than own if you only use it every so often), can make huge deposits into your savings account and really fast-track your goals.

Other Ways to Find Extra Money

A lot of the other ways to find extra money I've already talked about in other chapters.

Things like starting a side hustle to earn extra income, or ditching the car and biking or walking everywhere.

Living a simpler life is a great way to de-stress and build your savings at the same time.

I hope you've found some ideas and inspiration with the challenges and ideas I've included.

It isn't always easy to commit to building up your savings, but if you want to become financially independent you need to have money building up.

Always be saving.

Your future self will thank you.

———

TAKE ACTION

1. Automate the money that goes into your savings account.

A day or two after you get paid, transfer the majority of the allocated funds directly into your account.

2. Round up any small amounts and place those amounts into your savings too.

Small increments can add up. You can either do this

through a round-up feature at your bank (if it offers one), through a financial app, or do it yourself.

3. Create a savings challenge for yourself.

Either a 52-Week Savings Challenge, a Save Your Fives Challenge, or perhaps a Spending Equals Savings Challenge.

4. Add any extra lump sums, such as your tax refund, or other money you weren't expecting into your savings account.

Lump sums can provide easy boosts to your savings goals so that you can reach your goals sooner.

STEP FIVE - INVEST YOUR MONEY

What you'll learn in this section:

- An overview of what to invest in.
- Tips on investing in property.
- Ideas for starting a side business for extra income.
- Steps for investing in the stock market.
- Why you should always invest in yourself.

What To Invest In?

YOU'VE COME SO FAR.

You've got a good solid foundation with your money.

It's time to take that next step that is going to separate you from most other people and help you to truly become wealthy.

Don't be scared. You knew this chapter was coming. It's investing your money.

Investing is simply putting your money or time into something that will provide a return for you.

Now, when most people think about investing they think of the stock market. And for good reason. I personally think it's an excellent way of getting ahead financially, but it's also one of the riskiest ways to invest. With great returns can also come great losses if you invest in the wrong stocks or choose the wrong times.

While a later chapter in this book *will* be talking about the stock market (because that's what I'm most familiar with) there are also other ways to invest your money to start building long-term wealth. Many options that won't risk your hard-earned like the stock market might.

That may be property, business, or even investing in yourself with further education.

If some think investing is risky, I think relying on a paycheck over the long term is riskier.

Property Investing

Property investing is a passion for many investors. From buying low and selling high, to fixing up old properties to flip at a profit, or even buying an investment property to rent out to someone.

You can even take it and make it a huge business, owning a whole empire of buildings, either commercial or residential.

I'll be talking in more detail about property in the next chapter.

Investing in Business

Business is another option, although not without risks. You can dip your toe in slowly with a small side hustle or create a large business.

Businesses can be started with virtually no money these days, or you can invest in buildings or equipment and big ideas, side hustles right through to creating your own full-time job from home.

I actually think that everyone should start at least one business in their lives. Something that could potentially grow enough to replace their income.

Build Up Your Passive Income

The best investments are those that don't require a lot of your ongoing time.

That's the basis of passive income. You set something up once with either your skillset or money and then receive income from that source for months or years to come.

Cash flow is king, and the more sources of income coming in, the better it will be. That way, if one source dries up, there are more to replace it.

My expertise is in writing books that earn ongoing royalties. I write the book once and, hopefully, people like them enough to continue to buy them in the years that follow.

You could also build websites that earn affiliate or advertising commissions.

Or if you like real passive income, invest in dividend paying stocks. That requires very little of your time, but a lot of your money.

Investing for the Risk Averse

Even for the risk averse, keeping your money in high-interest savings accounts, and investing in yourself with education is still doing something to further your future.

There are many ways to invest and not all of them require the stock market.

Find something that you love doing that you can invest either your time or money into that will one day be enough to live on.

It doesn't matter what you choose. It just matters that you decide you're going to be smart with your money and your time.

That's how you win the wealth game.

———

TAKE ACTION

1. Think about what you want to invest in. Property, Business, Stocks?

There are many ways to invest and get a positive return.

2. Choose one thing to focus on.

Down the line, you can invest in multiple avenues, but to start with you need to focus your attention on just one thing for now.

The only time you're allowed to change that thing is if you get so good at it, it takes less of your money or energy, or it's such a complete failure that you have no choice but to move on.

3. Remember that there isn't a time limit.

You don't have to invest in anything right away.

If you're not ready, just think about what you'd like to do when you are. In the meantime, keep your money building up in your savings account.

Investing In Property

CASH FLOW (LEASING) VS CAPITAL GAIN (SELLING)

MANY PEOPLE ARE EXCITED about property more than the stock market. While the return on property is historically lower than the return on shares, the risk is also lower. There's no doubt that many people have made out very well by investing in property.

A house (or unit) is unlikely to go belly up like a company might making it a stable investment. Everyone needs somewhere to live. Property is going to be around for the long haul, excepting a catastrophe like a fire or a flood which you'll have insurance for anyway, right?

While I'm not as knowledgeable about the property market as the stock market, I know plenty of people that have made out very well.

There are three main ways that you can make money investing in property.

- Buying for one price and then "flipping it" (selling for a higher price).
- Renovating/remodeling so it increases in value to sell.
- Leasing it out to a tenant (residential) or a business (commercial).

Generally, you need some cash behind you to do this, but you can also borrow against your current property if you've built up enough equity to do so.

Loans for Investment Properties

There are two types of loans that you can take out when investing in property. A principal and interest loan, or an interest-only loan.

For your own home, it's a no-brainer. You choose the principal and interest loan so you can own your home outright when the loan ends.

But for investment properties, that isn't always the case.

A smarter strategy for investment properties is an interest only loan. Interest only loan payments are lower than principal and interest loans because you're only paying the interest portion of the loan back.

So if you're leasing the property, the payments should cover the cost of the loan, plus give you immediate cash flow to pay onto your own home and pay that off faster.

The exception is if you've already paid off your own home (or prefer to rent), then using a principal and interest loan on a residential property you rent out makes sense. It won't be as necessary on commercial property (as these tend to be about yield rather than capital growth), but for residential property, it's an option.

However, if you're flipping or renovating, you're only holding short term anyway, so the timeframe isn't long enough to build up equity. You want to pay the least amount on the loan as you can, which is why an interest-only loan is preferable.

Getting a Loan For Your Investment Property

Once you've found the property you want to invest in, you need to book a meeting with your bank to discuss loan options.

They'll approve or not depending on a few factors.

Mostly they'll want to know if you can afford to pay the loan if the worst happens (you can't get tenants or you can't resell the property). So you'll need to show that you have a stable income.

Other things they'll look at is property prices in the area to ensure that you're not overpaying. A good credit rating is another thing they'll look at. And of course, how much your assets are.

If you're approved, you can go ahead and start your property investment empire.

As your equity builds in your properties, combined with the positive cash flow, it will mean that you can afford to borrow for more properties. Why stop at one?

The type of property investment that you prefer depends on your goals.

Investing for Cash Flow (Leasing Your Property)

If you're interested in building up cash flow, then you want to choose an investment property that provides a good return.

The average rental return in Australia depends on

whether you choose to invest in a capital city or regional area.

Generally, the closer to the city you are, the less your rental return will be (but your potential for capital gain is greater). Currently in Australia, it averages around 3 percent p.a. yield, with Melbourne being the lowest at 2.89 percent (source: *https://www.businessinsider.com.au/australian-property-rental-yields-2018-1*).

Regional areas fare better with rental returns closer to five percent.

The USA has similar statistics.

The benefits of residential property aren't just the rental yield though, as the property will also be increasing in value over time.

Being a landlord of a residential property isn't the only way to get into the cashflow game though. You can also invest your money in commercial property—business owners need somewhere to rent too.

There are pros and cons of each type of property investment but here are the benefits (and pitfalls) of commercial property.

The first benefit is that rental yield is usually better. For commercial leases, it's common to get yields of around 10 percent p.a. (Source: https://www.corelogic.com.au/)

Commercial leases tend to be longer than residential, with businesses signing for three years and upward and staying for five to ten, as opposed to residential where the average tenancy is two years with people signing up for six months to one year at a time.

You can also get into the ground floor of commercial property for less money than residential.

For example, buying a car space in an undercover parking area in the city is less than a hundred thousand dollars investment, and you can earn rent on that space easily with virtually no maintenance or ongoing costs.

However not all commercial property is a good investment. Economic downturns can mean that your commercial property will be vacant for longer periods leaving you to cover costs, sometimes for up to a year or more.

Residential property does have good and bad years, but it's rare, unless there is something wrong with the property, to have long vacancies.

There also isn't much capital growth in a commercial

property like with residential. A house in an inner-city suburb has the potential to double in value every seven to ten years. That isn't the same with commercial property, which may only rise by a few percent.

Commercial property can be a good investment, but it's less about long-term capital growth and more about cash flow.

Investing for Capital Gain

The alternative for rental income is buying and selling for capital growth.

You can do this a number of ways, whether through flipping or renovating or just waiting for a strong market, but generally what you want is to sell at a higher price than you paid.

There are tax implications for selling investment properties in Australia. You'll be slugged with a Capital Gains Tax (CGT) based on the profit that you made. There are similar tax implications in other parts of the world too, so check with your accountant.

Tax costs aside, investing for capital gain is a fast way to gain good profits (assuming a good market) in nearly all parts of the country.

You just need to be prepared to wait or pretty up the property first.

Getting Into Property Without Actually Buying a Property

Don't have the cash, or the inclination to spend your Saturdays checking out what's available in the property market?

You might consider other ways to get into the property game without actually buying a building.

You can get started in the property market with very low costs if you're willing to pool your money with others.

Most micro investing apps are geared toward the stock market, but there are some that are using a similar concept for property too.

They'll take small amounts from you and a large pool of other people and use that to invest in either residential or commercial property. You'll reap the rental and capital gain rewards based on your share.

Another option is to invest in Exchange Traded Funds (ETF) that are exclusively property stocks only.

Technically that is investing in the stock market too, but

if your ETFs are strictly property, you could get away with calling yourself a property investor. It'll be the best of both worlds.

———

TAKE ACTION

1. Decide which property investment path you want to take.

Either flipping, renovating, or renting it out. Each have their pros and cons. Some require more capital, others more work.

2. Do your research on the properties in the area you're interested in to see if they fit with your goals.

That means looking online or heading out to open houses and inspecting the property yourself.

Find the property you want to invest in.

3. Take your financial information to the bank and apply for a loan for the property.

4. Once you own the property and either fix it

up, sell it, or get tenants, according to your goals.

OTHER OPTIONS:

If you don't want to, or can't afford, to get into property directly you can pool your money with others through property micro-investing apps. Research ones that are well reviewed and do your due diligence before committing your money.

Or, just buy a property only ETF through the stock exchange.

Investing In a Side Business

SIDE HUSTLES & SMALL BUSINESS

BRINGING in more than one source of income can mean the difference between just getting by and thriving.

I'm a big believer that everyone should look at building up passive income streams. That could be property or stocks or it could be that you start a small side business.

A side hustle if you will.

Side businesses don't have to be fancy or take up a lot of your time. You've probably heard of the more common ways to make some side income such as becoming an Uber driver or renting a room in your house through Airbnb.

There are even sites like TaskRabbit or Airtasker where you can find quick service jobs in your area. Jobs like mowing lawns or assembling Ikea furniture.

With technology today, it's possible to find many different odd jobs you could do for quick cash.

Digital Businesses

My favorite types of passive income businesses are digital because then you don't have to worry about inventory.

There are many ways to build positive cash flow passive income. Just by investing a small amount of time upfront you can reap the rewards for a long time afterward.

eBooks

My jam, which is obvious because you're reading this, is writing books. While I've been a writer since high school, and a published author for more than ten years, the world of publishing has now opened up to anyone with something to say or a story to tell.

These days you can reach an audience directly rather than going through a publishing company (although that way is still an option too).

If you can produce a professional product that people want to read, you can sell your book at all the major bookstores online.

Most bookstores take thirty percent of the cover price, leaving seventy percent for the author. You can also get print books done too if you want.

Write the book once and it'll sell for as long as people are interested in it.

Services

Not a writer? New authors are always looking for things like editors, cover designers, and marketers. All jobs you can do from home anywhere in the world.

Or you could become a virtual assistant for someone who needs emails answered or Pinterest graphics designed through sites like Fancy Hands.

Blogging

If you do like writing, there is also blogging, where you can earn affiliate income for recommending products. If you keep your blog authentic and recommend products you actually like and use, you can build a good business.

Blogs can also earn advertising revenue or brand sponsorship deals.

Don't want to build a website? You can become microblogger on places like Facebook and Instagram. Offer your opinions. Show people inspirational ways to live. Gain enough followers and the advertisers will show up.

Photography

Prefer to be behind the camera? If you're good at photography you can upload your photos to stock photography sites.

A popular photo can get the photographer good money for years to come.

YouTube

Or you might enjoy being in front of the camera on video. YouTube is still growing and is now the second largest search engine online.

Vlogging. Tutorials. Unboxings. You name it, there's money to be made just talking and doing your thing.

Fiverr

You can do almost anything on fiverr.com for five dollars

(actually four because Fiverr takes a $1 cut). Create a website banner, voice-over a message to someone, hold up a sign with a message on it.

Go and check some of the categories to get a feel if anything calls to you. Even a few things a week will add up to an extra $20 or $30 dollars for not a lot of time.

Courses / Classes

Knowledgeable about something? You could set up a course on Udemy or Teachable showing others how to do the thing you're good at.

You don't need to be an expert either. As long as you can walk a beginner through teaching them what they want to know, you've got enough knowledge to share.

Your Design on Physical Items

If you're good at graphic design, you can go with any of the companies that will sell your design printed on any manner of physical items like T-shirts or coffee mugs.

The company handles the printing, orders, and shipping and all you do is create cool images.

I know a graphic designer friend who designs typography quotes and uploads the design to a site where people buy coffee mugs or T-shirts with his design on it.

Physical Businesses

However, you don't have to limit yourself to digital products if you have skills in other areas.

Handmade Products

Are you good at making things? You could set up an Etsy store selling your bespoke handmade items. Bath bombs, cushion covers, bookmarks, jewelry, anything you can think of.

Courier

People like to get things with a click and a swipe these days. Become a courier for meals such as with Ubereats or deliver gifts and flowers.

Services

Go back to good old fashioned odd jobs like mowing lawns, cleaning pools, even cleaning whole houses.

It doesn't have to be manual labor though, your service could be tutoring school kids or offering pantry organization services.

THE MORE THINGS that you can find to do outside of your regular nine-to-five the better you will be because you'll have something to fall back on if something happens with your job.

Some businesses even make enough that you can quit your job. There has been many a millionaire made from the comfort of the kitchen table.

Invest in Yourself

And finally, always invest in yourself. Whether that's education or trying to be a better person.

Education doesn't have to stop at school. Learning from books, videos, or blog posts is easier than ever. Asking questions about something you want to learn of the right people can build skills and knowledge. A quick email is sometimes all it takes.

But the most important thing in which to invest? Building social skills and relationships. In fact, without friends and loved ones, all the rest is unimportant.

———

TAKE ACTION

Start a side hustle that either has the potential to become a full-time gig, or just to provide a few extra dollars a week.

Think about what skills you have that other people would need. Could you teach it? Create courses around it? Write a book about it? Show people how to do it on a blog or video?

Perhaps you could do jobs that others don't want to do, like gardening or cleaning. There is big money to be made for jobs people don't like.

Invest in yourself.

But most importantly invest in yourself. Always be learning and building important relationships with your loved ones.

Become Stock Market Savvy

INVESTING FOR GROWTH OR INCOME

IT WASN'T until I was in my twenties and discovered the stock market that learning how to build real wealth fell into place for me.

When I realized that anyone, even a regular single girl with a nine-to-five job, was able to invest in large billion dollar companies with just a small amount of money, I was hooked.

That's not to say I didn't make mistakes in the beginning. I did.

Once such mistake was investing in penny stocks. Low-priced stocks that only had to increase by a couple of cents for me to double my money. I quickly realized that low-priced stocks are low for a reason. I lost a few thousand to that education.

Eventually, I got better.

My early strategy for growth was (and still is) largely influenced by Warren Buffett's way of finding excellent companies for great prices.

I wrote about that experience in investing with my first book, *Shopping for Shares*. I wanted to create a guide to investing in the stock market for women just like me who wanted to get started but didn't know how. It was and still is my most successful book.

I followed that growth strategy for most of my investing, through good and bad years, but have recently shifted toward a more income producing one now.

Dividend income has become my new favorite way to invest.

I'll be talking more about that later in this chapter, but first, we need to go back to talking generally about stock market investing. Because there isn't just one place to start.

Getting Started In Stocks

Even if you don't wish to build a huge portfolio, I believe that investing some money into stocks will set you up well long term.

You don't need a lot of money to start, much less than people think, and you can learn as you go.

You can dip your toe into the stock market for as little as five dollars if you want. Not directly, since brokerage fees would negate any profit, but with any number of the new micro investing apps on the market right now.

You're lucky. It's easier than it's ever been to hold an investment portfolio.

Micro-investing Apps

Micro-investing apps can be a good starting point if you've never invested in stocks before.

They can whet your appetite for wanting to go deeper into investing or make you realize that the volatility of the stock market isn't for you.

The premise of most micro-investing apps is that you can add small amounts of your money into a pool of much larger money that then go into investing in (mainly) exchange-traded funds.

It creates a sort of forced savings investment portfolio.

In some of them, you can choose to round up your credit card purchases to the nearest dollar and invest the difference, or you can choose to automate regular amounts into the account (or both). Or you can choose which dollar amount you want to invest and leave it at that.

Most require a minimum balance such as five dollars to open and you'll get a choice of different investing options based on your risk preference.

It's an easy way to start.

Since most of them invest in Exchange Traded Funds, there will be ongoing costs, but the fees are usually reasonable (check their respective FAQ pages for exact amounts).

As a general rule if you keep your balance over $500 you should see returns.

I've dabbled with micro-investing apps, and while the experience has been positive, I prefer to invest directly.

Exchange Traded Funds (ETFs) Are a Good Starting Point

You can buy stock in hundreds of companies with one brokerage cost with Exchange Traded Funds (ETFs).

Diversifying your portfolio is the best way to lower your risk in the stock market.

It used to be that the only way to do that was to buy into more than one company, or hand your money over to a fund manager so they could do it for you.

Now you can do it yourself.

What are Exchange Traded Funds?

ETFs are index funds that are traded on the stock exchange just like regular stocks. Very similar to managed funds (mutual funds) that you'd buy through a fund manager.

Each exchange traded fund is different, but it's common that they have a mix of forty to two thousand different companies within each fund. So the beauty is that you can hold, perhaps, two thousand different stocks, just by buying the one fund.

Diversification made simple.

And ETFs pay you dividend income too. You can either

choose to take them as cash or reinvest them back into your investment, just like regular stocks.

Because you can trade them through your online stock-broker, they are very easy to buy and sell, unlike regular funds that usually require paperwork.

Also unlike managed (mutual) funds, you don't have a minimum amount that you have to buy. You could potentially buy just one share in the ETF if you wanted (tip: while you *could*, don't buy just one share).

Buying them on the exchange means that the price can fluctuate day to day, just like regular company stock. I have found that ETFs don't tend to be quite as volatile as many individual stocks though. That's because the nature of being an index fund smooths out the volatility of single companies.

That's not to say they don't rise or fall, you still need to do your due diligence.

ETF Fees

Even with ETFs, there is still a fund manager choosing the companies that go into that fund, and as such, there is usually a small yearly fee for management of the fund.

I've found with most ETFs I've looked at, that the fee is similar or less than that of a regular managed fund.

You don't need to pay for that separately though. It's absorbed into the profits of the fund. All you pay is the brokerage costs to buy and sell, just like any other stock.

Which ETFs?

There are hundreds of different types of ETFs trading on the stock exchange to choose from.

You could buy stocks from your country, from overseas companies, or mixes from all over the world. You can even buy ETFs for government bonds, property—both commercial and residential—and even currency funds.

So you could be a property investor by buying shares in a property-only ETF. I think that's cool.

And all for the cost of one brokerage fee.

Exchange Traded Funds are an Easy Way to Invest Overseas.

I've purchased stock in overseas markets before and I have to say, while it's possible to do from Australia, the brokerage fees for international stocks is costly, and the tax implications can be a headache.

I prefer buying ETFs in overseas companies than buying direct to avoid the unnecessary costs and paperwork.

So if you're keen to spread your investments to all corners of the globe, then stick with ETFs.

How To Survive Owning Stocks

The stock market can be a roller-coaster ride of highs and lows. Even those of us who have been investing for many years still feel the tugs of emotion when our portfolios move swiftly in any direction.

I equate it to stepping on the scales when you're dieting. That movement of the needle is either going to make your day or have you wanting to give up on your goals.

If you watch the market every day, like many people do, you are going to need a tough skin.

When stocks rise you'll feel like you're the boss and can't do a thing wrong. When stocks fall you'll dip into denial and be convinced that this investment thing is all a sham.

It's inevitable.

Having more money in the stock market only magnifies things. Even small fluctuations can look huge.

Keep a clear head.

If stocks are down, it's the value of your portfolio on that particular day that's decreased. You haven't actually lost anything (unless you sell, and don't). A paper loss is not an actual loss.

Same if stocks are up. You haven't made any money until you sell. It's just a number on a screen right now.

When to Buy Shares

You've saved up a few thousand and now you're ready to invest in the stock market.

While the best time to buy stocks is when they fall (some call it a crash, I call it the stock market going on sale), most of the time when you buy, it will be when you have the money to do so.

When you're ready:

- Open up a trading account. You only need an online trading account, not a full-service broker. Look for one that allows easy transactions and low brokerage fees.
- Spend time looking around the trading site. Find out how to place an order, how to sell. See what research tools they provide.
- Deposit your investment money into the

account required. Sometimes that's just your regular transaction account, other times you need to set up a specific trading account.

Unlike investing in ETFs, if you are buying single stocks, stick to those in your own country. The brokerage is expensive and tax implications of investing overseas can cause a headache at tax time.

So how do you choose which companies to purchase?

First, you need to figure out what you want from the stock market.

The two most common ways are investing for growth and investing for income.

Investing For Growth

Investing for growth or capital gain is what most people think of when they think of investing in stocks. It's where you buy at one price and over time want the price to go up so you can sell at a profit.

When looking for stocks to buy for growth you need to make sure that the company is stable and has good potential for the business to grow in the future.

Some of determining this is common sense. You

wouldn't purchase stock in a company whose business model is being taken over by technology, for example.

Other times you need to look at the company fundamentals. Fundamentals is just a fancy word for looking at the company's main financial details such as how profitable it is and what sort of return it will give investors.

You don't need a degree in finance or anything to determine which company is good though, you just need to look at a few things:

- Companies that have five years history on the Stock Exchange,
- The biggest companies by Market Capitalisation,
- Debt to Equity Ratio,
- Return on Equity (ROE), and
- Earnings Stability.

Let's look at these in more detail.

Companies With at Least Five Years History

The first thing to look at is to make sure the company you invest in has been around for the last five years. I prefer companies that have been around ten or more, but five is enough, especially in today's fast-moving technological environment.

The reason why is because you need some history to see if the company is sustainable long term. Most businesses fail within the first three years so if a company has surpassed that and is thriving, it's time to look at investing in it.

It helps to understand what the company does as well. That way you can make a judgment call whether it's a good long-term business. Is it likely they'll be around in another five or ten years?

Look at any stock chart to see if it has at least five years worth of data to determine how long it has been on the stock exchange.

Companies in the Top Indices

The next thing to look at is the biggest companies listed on the stock exchange.

That's those companies in the ASX200 in Australia or the S&P500 in the US (and equivalent in your country).

These are the companies with the biggest market capitalization.

This usually means they have enough money to grow and provide you, the stockholder, a share of those profits. (As long as they aren't coasting on borrowed money, which is the next criteria).

How Much Debt They Carry

I don't like companies that carry a lot of debt. Companies do need to borrow some money to expand and grow, but if their debt to equity ratios get above eighty percent I'll pass.

The reason for this is that if the company ever gets into trouble, it'll use its profits to pay off debts first and if the debts exceed the cash it has on hand, there won't be any left over to pay investors.

You can find this figure out in the risk section of the company research key measures page. It's usually called the Debt to Equity ratio.

Return on Equity (ROE) Above Fifteen Percent

A good measure of a healthy company is one where it's Return on Equity figure is fifteen percent or higher.

ROE is important for investors because it's a measure of the company's profits from the money that investors have put into the company.

You can find this figure on the company research financials page.

Earnings Stability

And the last thing to look for is earnings stability. This just means that year to year the earnings that the company produces is stable but growing. You don't want a company whose earnings fluctuate wildly from one year to the next as that won't lead to a healthy share price increase.

Earnings stability is usually on the company research key measures page.

How Many Stocks to Hold?

Once you find one company to invest in, start looking around for at least four more.

Five different companies is a good amount to aim for when starting your portfolio to get a good diversification mix.

Eventually, you can work your way up to about ten to twelve. That's all you really need for strong diversification.

Should You Take the Dividend?

When you are investing for growth, if you have the option, it's a good idea to re-invest the dividend. That way you'll be able to increase your holding without any extra effort or cost from you.

Investing For Income

Income investing also called dividend investing is where you choose companies based on the money they can give back to you in the form of dividends.

If you invest for income, you choose to take the dividend rather than re-invest it (because you want the cash flow).

The higher the yield, the more money you'll get in the form of dividend payments.

While not all companies pay out dividends, many do. They might pay four times a year, or more commonly in Australia, twice a year. If the company has had a particularly good year they might give out a special dividend to investors as a bonus.

When you decide to invest for the dividend income, you still want to look for a company with strong fundamentals, but it's the dividend yield that you'll be most interested in.

- Market Leaders,
- Dividend Yield at least 5% p.a., and
- Dividend Stability.

Let's look at these in more detail.

Choose Market Leaders

Just like with choosing companies for growth, when looking for companies for income, also stick with the market leaders.

That's those companies in the ASX200 within Australia, the S&P500 in the US, or the FTSE350 in the UK.

Dividend Yield

Look for a dividend yield that's more than five percent p.a.

You'll find that most good income stocks will land somewhere between five and ten percent. It's rare to find a company that pays above ten percent and if it does, it's generally not sustainable.

Find the dividend yield under income on the company research key measures page.

Dividend Stability

There are two parts to this criteria.

The first is that the company has been paying dividends for at least five years.

To make sure that the company consistently pays dividends, you need to have at least five years worth of history.

Again, like with growth, having a company that has been around at least five years or more shows that it has consistently paid investors and is likely to continue doing so in the future.

Check the dividend page of the company to find this out.

The second to thing to look for is to make sure that the dividend amount that the company pays is consistent and/or growing.

Have a look at how much the dividend payout for the company has been over the past five or more years to see how stable it is. If the amount is consistent year to year then it's a good buy. If it's growing each year, even by a small margin, then it's a great buy.

How Many Different Stocks To Hold?

Like buying for growth, it's a good idea to hold at least

five different companies to begin with. This spreads your risk and allows you to be receiving income at numerous times during the year.

Receiving Dividend Income Every Month.

It's possible to structure your portfolio so that you're receiving dividends every single month. It's a strategy that I've become increasingly interested in recently.

While it's not necessarily the most profitable way to set up an income-only portfolio (because you may sacrifice yield for a company that pays in a month that no other company does), the consistency of receiving regular income can be more important to some investors.

The concept is simple, you purchase shares in enough high-yielding companies so that each month at least one of those companies is paying you dividends.

In Australia where companies only pay dividends twice per year it's a little tricky. In a country, such as the US, where dividends are paid four times a year this would be easier to achieve.

Following is a list of high yielding companies in Australia and the months they pay dividends.

It isn't an exhaustive list, there are more you could find

and add, and of course, you would still need to do your due diligence before purchasing, but it will give you a good base from which to start.

(Australian Dividend Stocks, Using Stock Code, by Month)

- January - VHY, GEM, SCP
- February - SGP, CMW, CQR, GOZ
- March - WES, CWN, AIZ, PPT
- April - VHY, CBA, SPK, SUN, GNE, NEC
- May - CMW, BOQ, HVN
- June - AST, IFT
- July - VHY, NAB, WBC, ANZ, GEM
- August - SGP, CMW, CQR, GOZ, SCP
- September - WES, CBA, SUN, AIZ, PPT
- October - VHY, CWN, SPK, GNE, NEC
- November - CMW, BOQ
- December - NAB, WBC, AST, ANZ, IFT, HVN

Ex-Dividend Stock Price Fall

The stock price for dividend shares often follows a predictable pattern.

When dividends are announced, people will start to buy

that stock and the price will slowly increase. Generally, there is a sharp increase on the day before the ex-dividend date, and a dramatic fall after the ex-dividend date.

The fall usually corresponds to the approximate yield that the dividend is paying, so if the company is paying a three percent dividend, the stock price often falls by roughly that amount.

It's usually due to people trying to use a dividend stripping, or dividend capture strategy.

What is Dividend Stripping?

Dividend stripping is where people buy the stock solely for the dividend, but don't hold that company long term. They only hold for the minimum time allowed to get that dividend. Sometimes as little as one or two days.

They will make sure they own it on the record date (usually the day before the ex-dividend date) and sell on the ex-dividend day.

While it can be a profitable strategy, you still need to be careful. The price on the dividend day usually falls by the same amount that it's going to pay out so you don't want to make your money on the dividend, but lose it on the share price.

Also, if you want the tax credits, you need to hold for longer anyway. It's forty-five days in Australia and sixty days in the US.

After the ex-dividend date the stock price will slowly rise again (assuming the stock market is in a stable or rising market).

In my experience, it generally takes between two weeks to four months for the share price to fully recover or increase, again assuming a stable market.

It's worth knowing the ex-dividend date so you can predict the stock price fall. In a normal market, it will recover over the next weeks to months.

That is, until the next dividend announcement when the whole price cycle starts again.

Practice your New Year's Resolution to be Patient

Historically the stock market always goes up. If you look at any period in history, even the worst case scenario where someone has bought at the height of the stock market and paid the highest price and it's fallen the next day, it has always recovered.

You should always get the value of your portfolio back

eventually. It might take a few years if you've purchased at a peak time though, so you need to be patient.

If you've purchased for the dividend income, the stock price won't matter as much to you. You'll get paid the dividend no matter what the stock price is.

It's a reason why I've moved to an income-producing portfolio. I don't care what the market is doing because I'll always get paid the dividend. And if the company stops paying dividends for whatever reason, I'll sell and find another one that does.

Ignore the market. Pretend you don't own shares. Keep calm and carry on.

And don't sell in a bad market.

When to Rebalance your Portfolio

It's a good idea to rebalance your portfolio at least once per year. Even if you are investing for the long term, you need to check in to make sure that everything is still following the investment goals that you originally set for yourself.

Rebalancing is simply a case of selling those stocks you no longer want to hold and buying more of those that you do.

Most people rebalance at the start of the year or mid-year. But with a higher number of people and companies buying and selling at that time, you can end up with a price that's not in your favor.

Instead, choose a different day to rebalance your portfolio. Perhaps on your birthday. Most people won't be doing it on the same day as you so trading should be normal.

You won't need to rebalance more than once per year.

Constantly buying and selling has proven to give worse results than simply holding. Not to mention the brokerage fees for all those trades will kill your profits.

Once a year is enough, and if everything is still fine, you might not even need to change anything.

Don't Follow the Herd

Another important lesson I can give you when it comes to investing is to make your own decisions and don't get caught up in what everyone else is doing.

There is a herd mentality with making money (and especially stock investing) that creates crazy volatility.

You've probably seen it recently with cryptocurrency.

One person recommends it, more people jump in, and suddenly everyone is talking about it. It's the new cool way to make millions.

The only way to make money with such things is to get in early. People who became crypto millionaires bought years ago before anyone was interested. Once the herd jumped in they sold and got out. If there is huge buzz now, you've probably missed the opportunity.

And just like herds can make the price rise fast, they can make it fall even quicker.

I don't go for trends like that. I never invested in cryptocurrency because, by the time I knew about it, the wave was at its peak. I knew it was only a matter of time before it fell and lots of people would lose a lot of money.

When it comes to investing, don't go for crazy trends. Most of the time I don't have a clue what other people are doing.

I go about my research like I always have, and buy and sell when I'm ready.

Having said that, there is a way to take advantage of herd

mentality. It's called contrarian investing whereby you do the opposite of what everyone else does.

If everyone is selling, you buy. If everyone is buying, you sell.

Contrarian investing, if you have the stamina for it, can be extremely lucrative.

Some of the worlds richest people in the world such as Warren Buffett, Sir John Templeton, and more are highly respected contrarian investors. (Although Mr. Buffett likes to refer to himself as a value investor, first and foremost).

So trust yourself. Don't follow what others are doing. Do your due diligence.

That's the path to wealth.

———

TAKE ACTION

1. If you've never invested before start with Exchange Traded Funds.

They are a quick way of instant diversification and

someone else has chosen the stocks for you.

You buy ETFs through the stock exchange, just like regular stocks.

The Vanguard ETFs are good, but do your research before choosing which fund to invest in.

2. If you want to buy stock directly, first decide whether you're going to invest for growth or income.

If you're investing for growth, make sure to research:

- Companies that have five years history on the Stock Exchange,
- The biggest companies by Market Capitalisation,
- Debt to Equity Ratio,
- Return on Equity (ROE), and
- Earnings Stability.

If you're investing for income, look at:

- Market Leaders,
- Dividend Yield at least 5% p.a., and
- Dividend Stability.

To start trading, open an account with an online broker and get used to how to buy and sell via the platform.

Transfer money to the required account and make your first order.

3. Pretend you don't own shares.

Looking at the market everyday can mess with your mind. The daily fluctuations are not representative of investing over the long term.

Historically the stock market has always increased.

4. Rebalance your portfolio once per year.

Choose a date each each year to go through your portfolio and get rid of the companies you no longer want and buy those that you do.

OTHER OPTIONS

If you want to start small, look into micro-investing apps such as Acorns. You can build up your funds for investing through the app and get a feel for market volatility before committing to investing larger sums directly.

Continue The Journey To Wealth

CONCLUSION

THERE WE HAVE IT. The five steps to becoming wealthy.

1. Create a budget based on tracking your income and expenses.

2. Think mindfully about your shopping habits and see where you can cut back.

3. Make a plan to pay off your debts.

4. Start saving your excess money for something exciting.

5. Invest your money to make it grow faster.

Of course, it does mean that the hard work starts now if it hasn't already. But I know you're not scared of that.

You're inspired by the possibility of where you might end up.

I didn't know where I would end up when I started my own journey from virtually nothing to where I am now.

I didn't know who I would be.

What I discovered is that my life has changed immeasurably in some ways and hardly at all in others.

I'm still frugal, having been taught from a young age to be careful with money. I don't think that will ever change. Yet now I'm debt free and financially secure. That burden frees up the stress and worries from all those years when I did struggle. That is what has changed the most.

And that debt-free, low-stress life can be yours. You can make great changes to your life.

Most people underestimate just how much their lives can change in one year. Make that five or ten years, and you'll be in a very different place. A better place, if you work for it. The time is going to pass anyway, so why not do something about it?

Each step from this book builds on the previous to give you a blueprint that you can follow. Make your budget, control your spending, get out of debt, start saving, and invest your excess cash.

I've made it as straightforward and simple as I can.

Now it's up to you. I know you can do it. You've already accomplished so much.

Make that future better (and wealthier) for you and your family. You're worth it.

And lastly, thank you for taking the time to read this book. I truly hope it takes you from where you are now to a better financial future.

Because that will make my future better, knowing it helped or inspired even a little bit.

Let's go!

Tracey :)

ACTION PLAN

ALL THE STEPS

I THOUGHT it would be helpful to include all the action steps in one section so that you can flip here and refer to it whenever you need to.

STEP 1 - CREATE YOUR BUDGET

1. Decide whether you're going to use a spreadsheet, journal, or app for your budget.
2. The two most popular budget methods are the reverse budget and the zero-based budget. Choose whichever one you like best.
3. Put on music (it helps make it more fun).
4. Start the setup.

5. Make a section for income and add relevant rows for all your sources of income.

6. Make a section for expenses and add rows for your expenses. Group like things together if it makes sense to do so.

7. Fill in as much as you can but don't worry about making it perfect. You can tweak it as you go, add an extra row if you forgot something, or cross something out if you make a mistake. It'll take a few months to get it fully functional and work for you anyway.

8. For the reverse budget, pay any debts first then add money to your savings. Next pay your monthly expenses. You're free to spend what's left.

9. For the zero-based budget, allocate all of your money somewhere. Savings, expenses, or spending, etc. The goal is to make sure every cent is accounted for.

10. Keep updating it weekly as more expenses or income comes in. See where you are spending your money over time.

11. Stay motivated by finding inspiration with other books, images, or people in the same situation as you.

12. Automate your budget as much as you can to free up time for fun.

STEP 2 - CONTROL YOUR SPENDING

1. Face the fact that many people have a spending problem. We live in a world designed to make us spend money. Become more mindful of the constant marketing and advertising that try and make us feel unworthy unless we do/have something else.
2. Don't think spending is going to solve your problems. Spending is just a quick fix, not a long term solution.
3. Start a list of all tweaks and hacks you can make to your lifestyle that will result in you spending less but feeling better.

Things you can try include:

- Find cheaper alternatives (or dupes) of your favorite products.
- Try a no spend month, or week, or weekend.
- Give yourself a time-limit (say 24 hours) for impulse purchases.

- Work out your hourly rate and think of your purchases in terms of hours worked rather than the purchase cost.
- Unsubscribe from shopping emails.
- Avoid sales (unless you really need something).
- Cut expensive unnecessary items from your budget.
- Make your own food (and coffee) at home.
- Hack socializing with friends by not drinking as much or not eating out as often (choose home parties or midnight picnics instead).
- Wear simple timeless clothing.

STEP 3 - PAY DOWN DEBTS

1. Write down a list of all your debts. This can be in a spreadsheet program, a journal, or in an app.
2. Total it up.
3. Decide which method of paying off your debt you prefer. Choose either the Highest-Interest-Rate-First Method or the Debt Snowball Method.
4. Put your debts in order according to your

chosen method, i.e. lowest balance or highest interest rate.

5. Start a payment plan based on how often you get paid.

6. Once you've paid off your credit card, decide whether you're going to keep using it (responsibly), or if you want to switch to a debit card instead.

7. Create a points system complete with rewards for reaching certain 'levels' or amounts of debt paid off.

8. Start a calendar 'chain' system. Each week do something extra to pay off your debt. Mark your calendar if you complete your task. Don't miss a week.

9. Commit to not making any further debt.

10. Have confidence that you can do this no matter how long it takes, and if you can't that there are options available to you. But try for a year and see where you get before looking elsewhere. You might surprise yourself!

STEP 4 - START SAVING

1. Make saving a priority.

2. Know what you want to save for.
3. Commit to saving as much of your excess income as you can while still allowing yourself some discretionary income.
4. Simplify your bank accounts into two main accounts: a) Your regular everyday transaction account that your paycheck goes into. b) A high-interest savings account for your long-term savings.
5. If you haven't already, open your high-interest savings account and start saving.
6. Start your yearly expenses fund. Make a list of all your annual expenses and total it. Divide that number by how often you get paid.
7. Start an emergency fund. Save up an amount between $500 and $2000 depending on how much things cost in your area.
8. Automate the money that goes into your savings account to save time and have it increase on 'autopilot'.
9. If you want, create savings challenges for yourself.
10. Add any extra lump sums, such as your tax refund, or other money you weren't expecting into your savings account to help it build even faster.

STEP 5 - INVEST YOUR MONEY

1. Think about what you want to invest in. Property, Business, Stocks?
2. Choose one thing. Focus your attention on just one investment for now.
3. Remember that there isn't a time limit. You don't have to invest anything right away if you aren't ready.
4. **Property**: a) Do your research on the properties in the area you're interested in to see if they fit with your goals. b) Find the property you want to invest in. c) Take all your information to the bank and apply for a loan.
5. **Business**: Start a side hustle/job that either has the potential to become a full time gig.
6. **You**: Invest in yourself through education and/or relationships with others.
7. **Stocks**: a) Start with ETF's. b) Decide whether you want capital growth or dividend income. c) Research companies according to your goals. d) Don't watch the market (it's too volatile day to day). e) Rebalance your portfolio once per year.

About the Author

Tracey Edwards went from having zero savings to having enough money to give up her boring nine-to-five office job in just five years.

She continued her journey to wealth through both good and bad financial years to come out ahead.

With a degree in Journalism/Arts, she's determined to share her wisdom in easy to follow, no-nonsense guides, so you can share her success.

To find her online:

shoppingforshares.com
traceywritesbooks.com

youtube.com/traceysebooks

instagram.com/traceywritesbooks

facebook.com/tracey.edwards.author

Other Books By Tracey Edwards

30 Day Spending Detox

Shopping for Shares

$0 to Rich